George Washington, Spymaster

HOW THE AMERICANS OUTSPIED THE BRITISH AND WON THE REVOLUTIONARY WAR

THOMAS B. ALLEN

featuring illustrations by Cheryl Harness

NATIONAL GEOGRAPHIC
Washington, D.C.

For Norman Polmar,
a great friend and great companion in our search of spy stories.

✿ ✿ ✿

ACKNOWLEDGMENTS: This book was a mission for several secret agents who are
being revealed here with great thanks. My editor, Suzanne Patrick Fonda, slipped into the Library
of Congress one day and found the complete codebook prepared for Washington *(see pages
157–165);* I had found only a couple of pages. Special appreciation to Cheryl Harness, whose pen-
and-ink sketches provide new insights into events of the period. Bea Jackson took a time machine
into the 18th century and found type that George Washington would recognize. She also con-
spired with Susan Donnelly to produce the spy code puzzlers that sneaked into the book and its
jacket. I also want to thank Michael Warner and his sons, Tom, age 13, and Charlie, age 11, who
all read the book in galley form. And thanks to James H. Hutson, who provided another buried
treasure from the Library of Congress: information about Nathan Hale, written in the Revolutionary War era but unknown until the year 2000. Some spy stories take a long time to come
out of the secret world!

Book design by Bea Jackson. Production design by Dan Sherman.
Text is set in Caslon Antique.

HALF TITLE PAGE: Skull and Crossbones signify war between
England's crown and the Patriots with their liberty caps.
TITLE PAGE: General George Washington checks a map the night before a battle.
Unseen are the secrets he has learned through his spy network.

Library of Congress Cataloging-in-Publication Data
Allen, Thomas B.
George Washington, spymaster :
how America outspied the British and won the Revolutionary War /
by Thomas B. Allen ; featuring illustrations by Cheryl Harness.
p. cm.
Summary: A biography of Revolutionary War general and first President of the United States,
George Washington, focusing on his use of spies
to gather intelligence that helped the colonies win the war.
ISBN 0-7922-5126-1 (Hardcover)
1. Washington, George, 1732-1799—Career in espionage—Juvenile literature. 2. United
States—History—Revolution, 1775-1783—Secret service—Juvenile literature. 3. Spies—United
States—Biography—Juvenile literature. 4. Generals—United States—Biography—Juvenile
literature. 5. Presidents—United States—Biography—Juvenile literature. [1. Washington,
George, 1732-1799. 2. United States—History—Revolution, 1775-1783—Secret service.
3. Spies. 4. Presidents.] I. Harness, Cheryl. II. Title.
E312.66.A46 2003   973.3'85'092--dc21   2003006019

Printed in the United States of America

Table of Contents.

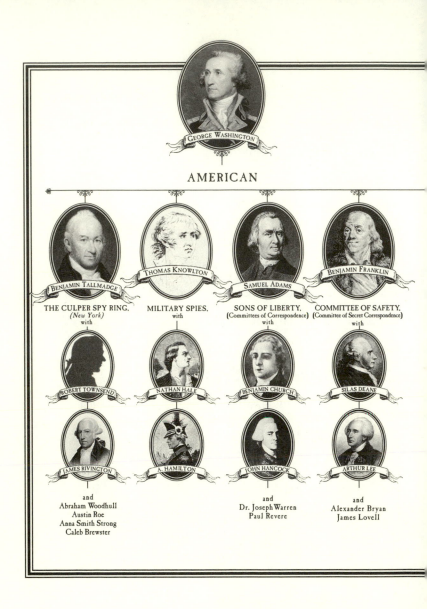

GEORGE WASHINGTON

AMERICAN

BENJAMIN TALLMADGE

THOMAS KNOWLTON

SAMUEL ADAMS

BENJAMIN FRANKLIN

THE CULPER SPY RING,
(New York)
with

MILITARY SPIES.
with

SONS OF LIBERTY,
(Committees of Correspondence)
with

COMMITTEE OF SAFETY.
(Committee of Secret Correspondence)
with

ROBERT TOWNSEND

NATHAN HALE

BENJAMIN CHURCH

SILAS DEANE

JAMES RIVINGTON

A. HAMILTON

JOHN HANCOCK

ARTHUR LEE

and
Abraham Woodhull
Austin Roe
Anna Smith Strong
Caleb Brewster

and
Dr. Joseph Warren
Paul Revere

and
Alexander Bryan
James Lovell

Spies of the Revolution.

NATHANIEL SACKETT

AGENTS,
with
John Honeyman
George Hewes
Hercules Mulligan
Elijah Hunter
(also spied for the British)
George Higday
and
Haym Salomon

JOHN JAY

COMMITTEE FOR
DETECTING AND
DEFEATING
CONSPIRACIES,
with
David Gray

JOHN CLARK

PHILADELPHIA
SPIES,
with
Lydia Darragh
"Old Mom" Rinker
Elias Boudinot

KING LOUIS XVI

FRENCH
INTELLIGENCE,
with
|

P. BEAUMARCHAIS

and
Julien-Alexander
Bonvouloir

KING GEORGE III

BRITISH

IN ENGLAND
Edward Bancroft
Paul Wentworth

IN AMERICA
John André
Benjamin Thompson
Nehemiah Marks
David Gray

IN FRANCE
Jacobus van Zandt
aka George Lupton

INTO THE WILDERNESS goes a mission led by George Washington (left). He was to find French troops and tell them to leave Virginia territory.

Chapter 1.

Birth of a Spymaster.

IN WHICH *George Washington*
learns a valuable lesson
in spying.

O n an October day in 1753, Robert Din-widdie, Royal Governor of His Majesty's Colony of Virginia, sat in his office in Williamsburg, the capital of Virginia, reading the latest reports from the frontier. The French were causing trouble again, pushing their way into British land. There was a whiff of war in the air.

Dinwiddie must have realized that Virginia's western boundary was fuzzy. Some Virginians even said that their colony stretched across the continent. But Dinwiddie knew that grand old claim was not realistic. He needed only turn to a map to see North America as it really was.

Thirteen British Colonies stretched along the Atlantic Coast from New Hampshire to Georgia, with a long piece of Massachusetts land called Maine in the north and, south of Georgia, a small piece of land called British Florida. Spain held the rest of Florida, along with most of the land west of the Mississippi River. The French occupied land in the Mississippi Valley called Louisiana and much of the land north of the Saint Lawrence River. They called that possession New France. If the French kept expanding their hold, they could link their southern lands with New France.

Dinwiddie believed that France was trying to keep the British colonists pinned to the Atlantic coast. Many British colonists, especially Virginians, wanted to move westward across the Appalachian Mountains. King George II, ignoring French claims to the Ohio River valley, had given permission for colonizing the area to the Ohio Company, a group of Virginia landowners and London merchants. Dinwiddie had sent a special message to London, advising that French troops had marched out of New France and built two forts in the Ohio Valley, land claimed by Virginia. On October 21 Dinwiddie received the king's answer: Order the French to leave British territory.

Dinwiddie was 60 years old and had spent most of his career collecting taxes, not shouldering a musket. He certainly could not go himself. Dinwiddie needed someone rugged enough to plunge into the wilderness, yet wise enough to deal with those clever French. Was there such a man?

George Washington was an officer in the Virginia militia, the small army that Dinwiddie controlled in the king's name. Washington had been made a major in February 1753, an amazingly high rank for a man who was not quite 21 years old. He was commander of the militia soldiers in southern Virginia.

Word of the French moves alerted the militia. When Major Washington heard about the royal orders to Dinwiddie, he rode into Williamsburg, sought out the governor, and volunteered for the mission.

At six foot three inches, Washington towered over Dinwiddie—and just about everyone else.

And he was powerfully built. Ever since his childhood on his father's Virginia farm, Washington had spent most of his days outdoors.

✧ ✧ ✧

George was 11 years old when his father died, ending his dream of going to school in England. At 15, he had another dream: He would fight at sea for England, which was then at war against France and Spain. His elder half-brother, Lawrence, who had been a British officer, saw to it that George was accepted as a midshipman in the Royal Navy. But before George could sail away to England, his mother objected. So George stayed home.

At the age of 16, George went off to live with his brother at Mount Vernon, Lawrence's Potomac River plantation. While living there, George did not get much schooling, but he did learn surveying—the mapping of the land. This was a needed service in the Colonies, where land was usually a wilderness without roads. After taking a seven-month course, George went to work.

Although he didn't know it then, George's adventures as a surveyor would prepare him for the rugged

OBEYING HIS MOTHER, George Washington gives up his hope of joining the Royal Navy. His younger brothers and sister witness his disappointment.

times to come in war. His diary tells of many days and nights in the wild during survey trips: "This day [we] see a Rattled Snake".... "we were agreeably sur-pris'd at the sight of thirty odd Indians coming from War with only one Scalp"... "Finding the River not much abated we in the Evening Swam our horses over." He slept under a blanket that held "double its Weight of Vermin such as Lice Fleas &c."

✧ ✧ ✧

By the time George Washington appeared before

5

SURVEYOR AT WORK: Teenager George Washington holds a surveying tool while a helper lets out distance-measuring chain and a slave looks on.

Dinwiddie, he was a major landowner. Lawrence had died the year before, and George had become the heir to Mount Vernon and the thousands of acres that his brother had owned elsewhere in Virginia. Dinwiddie had seen many a young man lose his lands and his fortune gambling at cards, but the governor knew that George was different. The governor's decision to send George off to deal with the French shows the trust that people already placed in young George Washington.

Dinwiddie gave Washington a letter to present to the French commander. It said that French troops were in British territory and must leave. The governor also gave Washington another mission: Get intelligence on the French. Find out how the French are turning Indian tribes against the colonists.

Washington left Williamsburg alone and headed west. All he knew was that the French commander was somewhere in the Ohio wilderness, about 300 miles from Williamsburg. His first move was to get a reliable guide. He headed for a small settlement called Wills Creek, where Christopher Gist lived. George probably had met Gist before, because Gist had worked for the Ohio Company, whose members included Lawrence Washington. Gist had explored the frontier wilderness along the Ohio River as far as where Cincinnati is today.

When Washington told Gist what the governor

wanted, Gist agreed to guide Washington. Gist was well known for the friendly relationship he had with Indians. [1]* Gist's knowledge of native languages would help when Washington wanted to talk to the Indians. But what about the French? George did not speak French and neither did Gist. So he went to Fredericksburg, Virginia, near his birthplace, to find his Dutch-born friend Jacob van Braam. Van Braam did not speak English very well, but he spoke French, and he understood what Washington wanted him to do. Although van Braam was not too enthusiastic, he agreed to act as Washington's French interpreter on the wilderness mission. (Washington was very good at persuading people.) Next, he hired four men who knew the wilderness. Two were traders friendly with the Indians Washington wanted to meet and question. Although he did not yet realize it, Washington was beginning to act like an intelligence agent: He found people who either knew what he needed to know or could find out.

Washington and the six men set out in "excessive

* Throughout the book, numbers in brackets correspond to numbers listed chapter by chapter in the Text Notes, beginning on page 167.

Rains & vast Quantity of Snow." After six days and nights of struggling on horseback through the passes of the Allegheny Mountains, they reached the forks of the Ohio (so called because that is where the Allegheny and Monongahela Rivers form the Ohio River, where Pittsburgh now stands). Because the "Waters were quite impassable" for horses, Washington sent three men along the shore and sped up his own journey by borrowing a canoe and taking the rest of the party by water.

At a nearby Indian village, Washington met with Half King, a powerful Seneca chief who hated the French. He had good reason, he said, claiming that Frenchmen had killed, cooked, and eaten his father. This must have come as a shock to the Virginia gentleman. But he calmly listened to Gist as he interpreted Half King's words. Washington gathered vital intelligence about the way the French were turning some tribes against the English and punishing Indians who would not aid the French.

Later, some of Half King's men took Washington to a house where a French flag flew. The French had taken over the house after throwing out the English trader who had lived there. When the French soldiers invited Washington to dinner, he eagerly accepted, hoping that he could get some information. And he got it, by listening patiently and taking little sips of his wine while the soldiers "dosed themselves pretty plentifully." The wine, he wrote, "soon banish'd the Restraint which at first appear'd in their Conversation, & gave Licence to their Tongues. . . .They told me, That it was their absolute Design to take Possession of the Ohio, & by G—they would do it."

The drunken Frenchmen also told Washington where their four forts were and that each one had about 150 soldiers in it. In response to Dinwiddie's order to leave the area, the French commander said that "the Country belong'd to them, that no Englishman had a Right to trade upon those Waters; and that he had Orders to make every Person Prisoner that attempted it on the Ohio, or the Waters of it."

The commander gave Washington and his men food and other supplies and sent them on their way. But before they left, Washington spotted many French canoes. Trying not to be obvious about it, he

SPYING ON THE FRENCH. Washington has his men quietly count canoes. He knows the fleet proves that the French plan to seize more Virginia land.

and his men counted the canoes, toting up "50 of Birch Bark, & 170 of Pine; besides many others that were block'd out, in Readiness to make." Washington believed that the French were building a fleet of canoes "to convey their Forces down in the Spring." He knew he had to get this information to Dinwiddie as soon as possible.

They started home by canoe. When rapids slowed their progress, Washington, determined to get his

AN INDIAN FIRES—AND MISSES. During Washington's trek into the Ohio wilderness, an Indian attacks him and his companion, Christopher Gist.

information to Dinwiddie swiftly, set out on foot with Gist. As the two men tramped through snow-covered woods, several "French Indians," as Washington called them, suddenly appeared. One of the Indians—"not 15 steps" away—fired a gun at them but missed. The other Indians fled as Washington and Gist "took this Fellow into Custody, and kept him 'till about 9 o'Clock at Night, and then let him go." Then they walked "all the remaining Part of the Night without making any Stop," hoping that the Indians would not begin pursuit until daylight. Washington had learned that colonists in the area recently had been killed and scalped, probably by Indians working for the French.

The two men struck out for the Allegheny River, planning to cross it on the ice. Finding the river only partially frozen, they built a raft and launched it— "but before we got half over, we were jammed in the Ice." Washington was thrown into the swift-moving water and saved himself by grabbing a log torn from the raft. He and Gist finally managed to wade ashore.

Scarcely taking time to dry themselves, they journeyed on. After 78 days in the wilderness they arrived in Williamsburg. Washington went immediately to Dinwiddie, who gave him one day to turn in a full report.

Working from his journal, Washington wrote a 7,400-word account. [2] Dinwiddie, who wanted aid from the king to stave off the French, had the report published. The publication made Washington famous in London as well as in the Colonies. His life as a public hero—and a secret agent—had begun.

AT THE CONTINENTAL CONGRESS in 1774, Washington, in uniform, appears with Patrick Henry (with glasses) and Richard Henry Lee.

Chapter 2.

Spy Against Spy.

*IN WHICH one group of spies
starts a revolution
while the other tries to stop it.*

Washington's report on the French plans
helped convince England to fight France
for control of the territory both nations
claimed. That struggle, known in America as the
French and Indian War, began in 1754, after Washington ambushed a small French force. [1] The
French counterattacked, defeating him at a hastily
built stockade near Great Meadows, Pennsylvania.
Washington named the site Fort Necessity.

Nearly a year later, French soldiers and their
Indian allies ambushed a large British unit led by

BULLETS CAN'T STOP HIM! In a fierce battle during the French and Indian War, four bullets riddle Washington's uniform—but do not strike his body.

General Edward Braddock north of Great Meadows. Washington was at his side. Although Braddock and his men knew little about the area, they had not tried to gather any intelligence on the enemy. So they were easily ambushed. Braddock was wounded and eventually died, along with about half of his men. "I escaped unhurt," Washington later wrote in a letter, "although death was leveling my companions on every side of me." He would later recall the lesson he had learned in that bloody valley: "There is nothing more necessary than good Intelligence to frustrate a designing enemy, & nothing that requires greater pains to obtain."

The French and Indian War dragged on until 1763. In the treaty that ended the war, France turned over all territory in North America east of the Mississippi River to the British. George Washington resigned from the militia with the honorary rank of brigadier general and returned home to Mount Vernon. His officers wrote of their regret that they had lost "such an excellent Commander, such a sincere Friend, and so affable a Companion." He would not be lost for long.

✦ ✤ ✦

Wars change people in ways that they do not see right away. During the French and Indian War, Washington and other people living in America thought of themselves as British, subjects of the king, and citizens of their colony. But by the time the long war ended, many people were calling themselves Americans. Those who were opposed to continued control by England called themselves Patriots.

The war cost England so much that George III,

who had become king in 1760, urged Parliament, England's law-making assembly, to find a way to pay for it. Parliament decided that since the money had been spent in defense of the Colonies, the colonists should pay for it. So in 1765 Parliament created a

new tax for the American Colonies. It was called the stamp tax because every time colonists bought a newspaper, calendar, marriage license, deck of playing cards, or pair of dice they had to pay extra for a special stamp.

TAX STAMP cost colonists two pence.

A member of Parliament, arguing against the stamp tax, said that the colonists, who had no representatives in Parliament, were being burdened with a tax they had not voted on. He called the colonists Sons of Liberty, a name Patriots adopted for an underground anti-England society. It would become America's first spy agency.

Many Sons of Liberty, sometimes called the Liberty Boys, were printers and publishers. They used their pamphlets and newspapers to spread propaganda—ideas helpful to their cause: "defense of the freedom that is our birthright." Propaganda can be one of the jobs of an intelligence service.

There were Sons of Liberty in cities in every colony. Most were craftsmen or ordinary workers. Some were lawyers and well-known citizens, such as Samuel Adams of Boston, a graduate of Harvard and cousin of John Adams, a future President of the United States. Sam Adams led the fight against "taxation without representation."

There were also Daughters of Liberty who played an important role in the campaign against the buying of products made in England. The young women among them were said to have vowed

ANTI-TAX "stamp" urges colonists to revolt.

not to marry a man who bought English-made goods. Some of these Sons and Daughters of Liberty would become part of the spy network that helped win the Revolutionary War.

Not all colonists were Patriots. Those who supported King George III called themselves Loyalists. Patriots called them Tories, an old British word for supporters of royal power. No one knows how many

Tories there were in the Colonies. Some historians believe that about one-third of the colonists were Tories, one-third were Patriots, and the rest didn't take sides. The threat of rebellion spread as the Liberty Boys and other Patriot groups gained followers.

PATRIOTS haul a Tory (a pro-British colonist) up a "Liberty Pole."

The man in charge of trying to keep order was General Thomas Gage, commander of all British troops in North America. Gage was well aware that Patriot propaganda was fanning feelings of revolution. So he ordered the Secret Service, an intelligence agency run by the British Army, to spy on the Sons of Liberty. The Secret Service put counterspies—spies who hunt and trap other spies—into the Sons of Liberty, especially in New York and Boston. Meanwhile, the Sons planted their own spies wherever they could. America was an ideal place for the dangerous game of spy vs. spy. People on both sides spoke the same language and could easily make believe they were Tories or Patriots.

Gage didn't need spies to know that Boston was a trouble spot. Fiery Samuel Adams, backed by the Massachusetts House of Representatives, called on all the Colonies to disobey British tax laws. In response, the British governor of Massachusetts closed down the legislature, and Gage ordered more troops from England. Hundreds of British soldiers landed from Royal Navy warships. People gathered at the docks and yelled: "Go home, Redcoats!"—or made fun of the "Lobsterbacks" stiffly marching to their camp on Boston Commons.

Boston papers published false or exaggerated propaganda stories about attacks on citizens by Redcoats. Gangs of men and boys, egged on by the Sons of Liberty, shouted insults at soldiers. On March 5, 1770, Crispus Attucks, a former slave, was in the front rank of an angry crowd facing several British soldiers armed with bayonet-tipped muskets. A couple of the colonists began throwing snowballs. The British started shooting. When it was all over, Attucks and two others lay dead; two others died later from their wounds.

THE "BOSTON MASSACRE," as Paul Revere made it look in his engraving (above), shocked colonists. But juries, judging facts, found Redcoats not guilty of murder. John Adams was a lawyer for the soldiers.

For a long time there had been only propaganda and secret deeds. Now there was blood on the cobbled streets. Adams called the shooting the "Boston Massacre." In the *Boston Gazette,* Paul Revere, a well-known silversmith—and a Son of Liberty—published a poem, along with a drawing showing a British officer raising his sword to order his soldiers to fire on the crowd. The drawing was pure propaganda.

The officer had not ordered his soldiers to shoot.

But the propaganda worked. Soon afterward, the new taxes were stopped—except for a tax on tea. Angry Sons of Liberty stepped up the campaign for independence. One of their targets was the royal governor of Massachusetts, Thomas Hutchinson. In June 1773 the *Boston Gazette* published letters that Hutchinson had written secretly to his superiors in England urging that more troops be sent to Boston and that the colonists deserved to lose some of their civil rights. Thanks to the Sons' propaganda network, the content of the letters was revealed in newspapers throughout the Colonies. Hutchinson fled to England. The man who had leaked the explosive letters was Benjamin Franklin, who would become one of America's most important secret agents.

COFFIN image from a newspaper bears the initials of Crispus Attucks, killed in the "Boston Massacre."

Throughout the Colonies, Patriots organized Committees of Correspondence. One of the most active was in Massachusetts. Founded by Sam

Adams, its members included John Hancock, a businessman and a smuggler, and two doctors, Benjamin Church and Joseph Warren. One of the three, we know now, was a British spy.

These committees, just like modern intelligence agencies, operated openly by holding anti-tax meetings or printing propaganda and secretly by running spy networks. They kept the Colonies in touch with each other through secret correspondence and later would help make united action possible.

In an event staged by Sam Adams on the night of December 16, 1773, a group of about 60 Patriots dressed as Indians swarmed onto three ships and dumped 342 chests of British tea into Boston Harbor. Outraged, the royal governor closed the port to all trade, threatening the people with starvation until they paid for the tossed tea. King George put Massachusetts under military rule and made General Gage governor.

News of the British reaction to the "Boston Tea Party" spread as "express riders" carried letters to and from Committees of Correspondence. Massachusetts wasn't the only colony where trouble was brewing. When Virginia's royal governor shut down the House of Burgesses, George Washington and Patrick Henry were among the representatives who urged all the Colonies to send delegates to what they called a "Continental Congress" to plan what to do next.

Delegates from every colony except Georgia began meeting in Philadelphia in September 1774. One of the delegates' first acts was a decision that "the doors be kept shut" and that "the members consider themselves under the strongest obligations of honor, to keep the proceedings secret."

Both the British and the Patriots believed that a shooting war was almost sure to start at any moment. Spies from both sides

THE BOSTON TEA PARTY.
Patriots, disguised as Indians, dump tea into Boston Harbor in an anti tax protest.

were sniffing around, trying to find out what the other side was up to. In Boston the Sons of Liberty met regularly at the Green Dragon Tavern. At each meeting every man swore on a Bible that he would keep the Sons' secrets. But one day a man who was *not* a Liberty Boy told Revere everything that had been said in the tavern the night before. In modern spy talk, his warning meant there was a mole—a spy who works inside the enemy's intelligence agency— in the Sons of Liberty! Thanks to this mole, General Gage knew what the Sons of Liberty were planning.

From his own Secret Service, Gage sent two officers disguised as "countrymen" to find out about a store of guns and gunpowder that the Patriots reportedly had in Worchester, Massachusetts. Their cover was blown when an African-American woman who was waiting on them in a local tavern recognized one of the men as a British officer from Boston. [2] The two spies had better luck in Concord, where they learned that the Patriots were grinding meal into flour for soldiers' rations and were storing "powder and cartridges."

On April 6, 1775, Gage's mole in the Sons of Liberty reported that he had seen four stolen British cannon and other weapons in Concord. The spy said a "sudden blow" would stop the rebels. Gage agreed. Based on reports from his spies, he drew a map that showed the location of the Patriots' arms and supplies and ordered an attack.

Events were moving rapidly. On the night of April 18, 1775, Dr. Warren of the Massachusetts Committee of Correspondence told Paul Revere that the committee had learned about a secret British plan: Redcoats were going to seize the weapons stored at Concord. Along the way, they were also going to arrest Samuel Adams and John Hancock, who were staying in a Patriot's home in Lexington.

The Sons of Liberty had worked out a plan of their own that they hoped would allow Revere and another rider, William Dawes, to reach Lexington first and warn the Patriots. When Revere learned that two lanterns had been hung in the bell tower of Boston's Christ Church, he knew it was a signal that the British would be coming "by sea" (meaning across the Charles River) and then marching to Concord. He and Dawes took off before the troops came ashore.

In the first minutes of April 19, hundreds of British troops left Boston, crossed the Charles River, and marched toward Concord. Meanwhile, thanks to Revere and Dawes, church bells rang and muskets

PAUL REVERE'S RIDE takes him to Lexington, where he warns Sam Adams (far side of the table) and John Hancock (holding gun) that Redcoats are coming to capture them.

fired—warning signals from the Patriot network that the British were coming. At Lexington, about halfway to Concord, the Redcoats saw about 70 militiamen lined up on the village green. Someone, still unknown, fired the first shot. The Redcoats fired a volley and charged with bayonets, killing eight Americans.

The Patriots' spy network saved Adams and Hancock from the British. But near Concord a British patrol held Revere for a time and took away his horse. Back in Boston, Revere's wife, Rachel, was worried. She wrote a letter, put it in an envelope along with some money, and handed it to Dr. Church, a member of the Committee of Correspondence. He was to give it to Paul whenever and wherever his mission ended.

As the British marched on to Concord—rank on rank, as if on parade—the Patriots' spy network mustered hundreds of militiamen. [3] The Redcoats, a British officer later wrote, were suddenly under "heavy fire from all sides, from Walls, Fences, Houses, Trees, Barns, etc." Surprised by such warfare, the British troops retreated toward Boston.

Express riders carried the news of the Massachusetts battles to the Second Continental Congress, which was meeting in Philadelphia. Suddenly faced with having to run a revolution, the delegates all turned to the one man who could take charge. They named George Washington Commander-in-Chief of the Continental Army. It would only be a matter of time before he also became the secret spymaster of the Revolutionary War.

WASHINGTON TAKES COMMAND of the Continental Army on July 3, 1775. The artist gives the ragtag army imaginary uniforms and weapons.

Chapter 3.

A Spy
Must Die.

IN WHICH *spies on both sides*
are discovered, caught,
and hanged.

Washington took charge of the rebel army at Cambridge, Massachusetts, on July 3, 1775. Made up of about 15,000 men, it had little ammunition or other supplies. He knew he would need more than this to beat the British. Within two weeks of becoming commander-in-chief, Washington began his career as a spymaster. On July 15, 1775, he paid $333.33 to an unidentified person "to go into the town of Boston; to establish a secret correspondence for the purpose of conveying intelligence of the Enemys movements and designs."

(That was a large payment; $333 in 1775 would buy about what $7,600 would buy today.)

Both Washington and General Gage desperately needed information. Soon after taking command, Washington had seized Dorchester Heights, overlooking Boston. He had enough troops to keep the British in Boston, but he did not have enough men or ammunition to take the city. So he laid a siege, surrounding the city so that the British couldn't come and go. Washington's siege would last for nearly a year. Gage, unwilling to attack the besiegers, waited for reinforcements from England. Would the rebels attack? Was help for the Redcoats on the high sea, heading for Boston? Spies for both sides made their way in and out of the city seeking answers.

Espionage tricks were also going on elsewhere. One day Gage received a letter from James Wright, the royal governor of Georgia. "No danger is to be apprehended," Wright wrote, saying that revolution had not flared up in Georgia or "in the proceedings or designs of our neighbors of South Carolina." Gage was relieved; he did not have to worry about those two colonies.

KEEPING AN EYE ON THE BRITISH, General Washington
watches ships in Boston Harbor from Dorchester Heights. Threatened by Patriot
cannon on the high ground, the British leave Boston.

But the letter that Gage received was *not* the
letter that Governor Wright had written. Patriots
had somehow managed to intercept the real letter,
in which Wright had warned that the rebels were
threatening British rule. Wright had also written to
Admiral Thomas Graves, Gage's naval commander,
asking for "immediate assistance" and "a sloop of
war of some sort." Patriots changed that letter to

say, "I now have not any occasion for any vessel of war." The Patriot forgers had also closed the letters with perfect copies of the governor's royal seal. Eventually, Wright discovered the forgeries, but the Patriots' trickery kept British gunboats away long enough for the revolution to take hold in Georgia. Although there is no direct link between this incident and spymaster Washington at that time, later in the war he would often use such tricks.

Gage kept a close watch on suspected Patriots in the besieged city. But, to put fish on Boston tables and to feed his troops, he had to allow fishermen to go to sea. Some of those fishermen looked for more than fish. One of the spying fishermen was George Hewes. He had been in the crowd involved in the Boston Massacre and later took part in the Boston Tea Party. He sold fish to the sailors of the British fleet in Boston Harbor for nine weeks, then slipped into Lynn, a port about ten miles northeast of Boston, and was taken overland to Washington's headquarters in Cambridge. There, Washington, after getting all the information that Hewes had obtained, invited his agent to dinner. [1]

Although Washington was getting bits of intelligence from agents in Boston and from the Sons of Liberty, he still did not have an organized spy network. Nor did he have a counterintelligence organization to search out moles. He learned his first lesson about the necessity of counterintelligence when a young woman was brought before him for questioning about a coded letter she had been given.

Washington was told that a baker had been given the letter by the woman, a former girlfriend. She asked the baker to deliver the letter to the captain of a Royal Navy warship off Newport, Rhode Island. When the suspicious baker and a Patriot friend opened the letter, they saw that it was in code. Believing that the letter was somehow involved in British spying, they turned it over to another Patriot. He got it into the hands of American officers who passed the letter and the woman's name to Washington.

"I immediately secured the woman," Washington later wrote. He began questioning her and "for a long time she was proof against every threat and persuasion to discover the author."

Finally, she broke down and named the writer of the coded letter: Dr. Benjamin Church.

Washington was shocked. Church was a trusted Patriot, a tea tosser at the Boston Tea Party, a Son of Liberty, and an adviser to the Second Continental Congress. He had treated the wounded at Bunker Hill. Washington had just made Church the chief physician of the army, at a salary of four dollars a day.

SEEKING THE TRUTH from a suspected spy, Washington gets shocking news about a "mole."

Church a traitor? Washington needed evidence. He sent officers to Church's home with orders to bring him every piece of paper showing that Church was a spy. They found nothing, leading to suspicions that there was another British spy in their ranks who had got to Church's house before them. That spy was almost certainly Benjamin Thompson, whose reports in invisible ink were found long afterward. When the British finally evacuated Boston, Thompson fled to England, leaving his wife and small daughter behind.

To find out what was in the letter, Washington

called in James Lovell and two other amateur code-breakers. They produced two identical solutions: The letter, addressed to General Gage, contained reports on Washington's military plans and on the strength of the Continental Army.

Washington wanted to punish Church. Hanging was the time-honored fate of convicted spies, but Church could not be executed by hanging or by any other means because Congress had not yet passed any laws about treason or espionage. Washington decided that he, as commander-in-chief, had the power to have a kind of military court called a court martial. So, as the head of the court martial, Washington weighed the evidence and listened to Church, who claimed he was innocent. Washington found Church guilty of "criminal correspondence with the enemy" but did not go so far as to convict him of espionage. Congress ordered Church put in a Connecticut prison. Later, claiming illness, he got himself confined in Massachusetts. Finally, around 1778, he was allowed to sail to the West Indies. His ship was lost at sea.

We now know that Church had been spying for a long time. [2] He was especially active in the weeks before the battles of Concord and Lexington, when he gave General Gage information about the Patriots' preparations for revolution, including plans to build fortifications on Breed's Hill. (On June 16, 1775, about 1,000 Americans held off 5,000 British troops until, exhausted and out of ammunition, the ragtag army retreated, leaving behind 226 British dead and 828 wounded on what is now usually called Bunker Hill.) Remember the letter that Paul Revere's wife, Rachel, gave Church? He passed that letter on to Gage—and he never gave Rachel's money to Paul Revere.

✤ ✤ ✤

On March 17, 1776, as the siege of Boston neared a full year, the British left the city on ships that sailed for Halifax, a safe port in British Canada. There they would reorganize and wait for more troops from England. Washington marched into Boston, liberating the city, and then led most of his army to New York City. There Washington would begin setting up his biggest and most successful spy network.

Washington would hold New York only for a

short time. The city was a stronghold of Tories. Most of them were merchants who saw the war as an annoyance that interfered with trade. A few Tories, though, were determined to strike a blow for the king—by killing or kidnapping George Washington. Rumors of murder plans swept the city. According to one rumor, Washington had pushed away a plate of peas, a favorite food. When the peas were fed to some chickens, they died. A snitch helped to expose the kidnapping plot.

POISON VICTIMS.
Chickens promptly die after eating some peas that had been rejected by George Washington.

Sometimes people pass on information to help get themselves out of trouble. They are snitches, not spies. But their information becomes intelligence. Isaac Ketcham, a smalltime criminal, was a snitch. While in a New York jail, he overheard a fellow convict boasting about being a member of a gang plotting to kidnap Washington. The boastful convict was Sergeant Thomas Hickey, one of Washington's bodyguards. Hickey was in jail for trying to spend counterfeit money. Ketcham secretly let the jailers know that he had important information to trade for his freedom.

That information led to Hickey's court martial for "mutiny, sedition, and treachery." Washington, who presided over the court, found Hickey guilty and ordered him hanged as "a warning to every soldier in the Army." [3] Probably to keep others from getting similar ideas, no mention was made of the kidnapping plot.

Two days after Hickey was hanged, British troops landed on Staten Island, in New York Bay, a few miles from Washington's headquarters. Washington knew he had to organize Patriot networks to spy on the Redcoats in New York. First, though, he needed answers to the kinds of questions that a general needs as he prepares for battle: Where are the enemy soldiers? How many are there? What are they planning to do?

Washington wanted a special operations unit made up of volunteers who could both fight and gather intelligence "by water or by land, by night or by day." For the commanding officer, Washington picked Lieutenant Colonel Thomas Knowlton, a veteran of the French and Indian War and a hero of Bunker Hill. The volunteers called themselves Knowlton's Rangers. [4] One of the rangers was Captain Nathan Hale, a 21-year-old former teacher from Connecticut.

When Washington asked for an officer to go behind British lines and spy on the enemy, the first man Knowlton asked showed him what a typical soldier thought about spying: "I am willing to go & fight them. But as far as going among them & being taken & hung up like a dog, I will not do it."

Nathan Hale then spoke up: "I will undertake it."

From what we know of his mission, Hale slipped behind British lines on Long Island, saying he was a schoolteacher—a natural "cover." Little has been known about his capture. But, according to a newly discovered account, Hale was tricked and seized by Major Robert Rogers, a bold British officer known for his cunning. Rogers was searching in Long Island ports for Tory recruits when he spotted Nathan Hale as a probable spy. Rogers, switching to civilian clothes, claimed to be head of a ring spying on the

A SPY'S FATE awaits Nathan Hale, who was captured by the British and hanged as a spy. His body was placed in an unmarked grave.

British and got Hale to admit that he also was a spy—with members of Rogers's "spy ring" as witnesses. As Hale relaxed with his newfound friends, he was arrested. He tried to change his story. But it was too late. [5]

He was sentenced to death without a trial. British officers would not allow him a Bible or a visit from a clergyman. Just before the hangman's noose was put around his neck, Nathan Hale said brave words. According to tradition they were: "I only regret that I have but one life to lose for my country."

The history of Revolutionary War espionage was changed by the deaths of Nathan Hale and Knowlton, who was killed in battle before Hale's execution. With Knowlton dead, Washington had no way of knowing exactly what went wrong in the planning of Hale's mission. Washington was not a man who let failure get in his way. He came up with a new idea: Instead of relying on officers to gather military intelligence, he would do what the Sons of Liberty had done in Boston. He would use civilians—sharp-witted Patriots who could spy while making believe they were Tories.

The Redcoats drove the Continental Army from New York in September 1776 and would hold the city throughout the war. During all that time, however, Washington constantly received information about British activities in New York, thanks to Patriot spy networks in New York City and on Long Island. And he himself would become part of a spy ring that would help him win the war.

COMMANDER-IN-CHIEF George Washington is a soldier in public and a spymaster in secret. He runs agents, reads coded messages, and watches for moles.

Chapter 4.

George Washington, Agent 711.

IN WHICH
*the general sets up
a spy ring.*

I n December 1776 Washington's battered army, driven from New York, was scattered along the Pennsylvania side of the Delaware River. On the New Jersey side, guarding Trenton, were Hessian soldiers hired by the British. The main British Army was spending the winter in New York. Old World armies did not fight in the winter; New World armies were expected to do the same. But Washington was desperate. He knew that his troops—and Congress— needed a victory. "I think the game is pretty near up," he wrote his younger brother on December 18.

Washington's ragged soldiers were surprised by an order that came from the general himself: Find and arrest a Tory named John Honeyman, a man hated by his New Jersey neighbors as a British spy and traitor. Why was Washington bothering with one of New Jersey's many Tories? Didn't he know that what the army really needed was a chance to win a battle?

Honeyman sold meat to the British and to the Hessians, so called because they came from the Hesse region in what is now Germany. Honeyman, who had fought heroically in the French and Indian War, told everyone that he was still loyal to England. And his loyalty was good for business now that the British were in control of the area. He never sold meat to the ever-hungry American soldiers.

On December 22 American soldiers on patrol spotted Honeyman, a big man with a cattle whip in his hand. After a chase and a whip-cracking scuffle, they wrestled him to the ground. At gunpoint, Honeyman was brought to the farm that was Washington's headquarters. The general sternly ordered the soldiers to leave him alone with Honeyman. If he tried to escape, he said, they should shoot to kill.

After a while, Washington called in the soldiers and told them to lock Honeyman up until the next day, when he would be put on trial as a spy. But that night a haystack somehow caught on fire. Honeyman's guards ran to fight the fire, and Honeyman escaped.

He crossed the river, found his way to the Hessian encampment at Trenton, and told the commander, Colonel Johann Rall, that he had no reason to fear an attack from the Americans. They were "an army of farmers" too hungry to fight. Rall laughed and started talking about the Christmas party he was planning. There would be a large meat order....

Early on the day after Christmas, Rall and his men were sleeping off a long night of celebrating. Suddenly, Washington's men appeared. They had crossed the icy Delaware River in scores of boats that Washington had hidden away. In a battle that lasted less than an hour, Rall and 106 other Hessians were killed; four Americans were wounded. The army of farmers seized Trenton and later proudly paraded some of their 900 Hessian prisoners through the streets of Philadelphia. The game, as Washington had called it, was not up. The Revolution had scored a victory.

For a long time, no one knew how Washington the spymaster had aided Washington the general. While Honeyman was selling meat to the British and Hessians, he was gathering information—the location of camps, the number of troops, the roads without sentries. Washington had made him an agent long before, ordering him to pose as a Tory and to stay with the main British forces as they moved across New Jersey. Washington, of course, arranged for Honeyman's "escape" after getting his report. In modern spy talk, Honeyman was a "sleeper," an agent under cover in enemy territory and awaiting orders, usually for a single, vital mission.

When Honeyman's Patriot neighbors in Griggstown, New Jersey, heard about his escape, they rushed to his home and threatened to burn it down. Honeyman's wife, Mary, handed the leader of the mob an official-looking paper. It said that Honeyman's wife and children were to be "protected from all harm" even though they were kin of "the notorious Tory, now within the British lines and probably acting the part of a spy." The paper was signed by General Washington. [1]

ANGRY NEIGHBORS threaten to torch John Honeyman's New Jersey home. What they don't know is the man they call a traitor leads a double life: He spies for George Washington.

Washington, by personally running Honeyman, acted as a "case officer." But he realized that he could not do this with all of his spies, so he put an army officer in charge of the civilian spies.

Washington chose Major Benjamin Tallmadge, who had been a close friend of Nathan Hale and, like him, had taught school in Connecticut. Tallmadge, a bold and dashing officer, would run what today would be called a department of military intelligence.

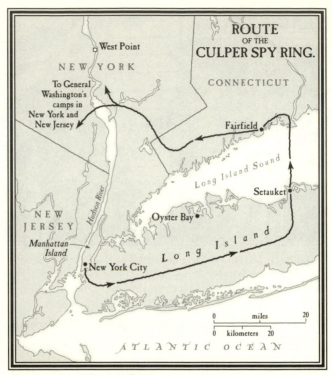

SPY HIGHWAY of the Culper Ring uses land and sea routes to avoid Royal Navy ships and Redcoat patrols on shore.

Tallmadge, according to one of his soldiers, "was a large, strong, and powerful man and rode a large bay horse which he took from the British. He was a brave officer, and there was no flinch in him. He was a man of few words, but decided and energetic, and what he said was to the purpose."

Tallmadge eagerly went to work, perhaps because he wanted to avenge the death of his friend Nathan Hale. Like Washington, Tallmadge had no espionage training and had to learn on the job.

Washington knew where most of the work would be done: New York City, headquarters of the British Army. He ordered Tallmadge to set up a spy ring that would provide such important secrets as the size and location of British military supplies and "the health and spirits of the army, navy and City." In another spymaster order, he said he wanted only "the naked facts without comment or opinion."

Tallmadge had been born on Long Island, which, like New York City, was occupied by the British. He began setting up a spy network by turning to trusted friends. One of them was Abraham Woodhull, who lived in Setauket, on Long Island Sound, across from Connecticut. Tallmadge gave Woodhull a "cover name" (Samuel Culper), the name by which others in the ring would know him.

In a well-run spy ring, people do not know each

other's real names. And agents try to stay separate from each other. If one is caught, he or she does not know the true identities of the others. Tallmadge never revealed anything about the way he ran his agents. In his manuscript about the war, he only said, "I opened a private correspondence with some persons in New York...." [2]

Washington knew exactly what he wanted of each agent: A person who could "mix as much as possible among the officers and Refugees [Tories] visit the Coffee Houses, and all public places." Washington preferred agents who "live with the other side; whose local circumstances, without subjecting them to suspicions, give them an opportunity of making observations."

Washington designed his intelligence system so that he could run his own agents, as he had run Honeyman. Or, he could have Tallmadge run agents as a case officer. Tallmadge was connected to Washington and to his own agents—*but the agents were not connected directly to Washington.* Tallmadge told Washington what the agents found out. But Tallmadge did not tell Washington the names of the agents. All Washington knew was that there was an agent Tallmadge called Culper Sr. (Abraham Woodhull) and an agent he called Culper Jr.

Culper Jr. was Robert Townsend, a merchant in New York City—a perfect cover because he could travel to and from Long Island on business. And he was a Quaker, a religion that was against war. (British counterintelligence officers thought that Quakers would not support revolution against the king.) Townsend also added to his cover by joining a Tory militia and writing anti-Patriot articles for the *Royal Gazette,* a pro-Tory newspaper.

James Rivington, the man who printed the *Gazette,* was one of New York's best known Tories. Patriots despised him. Before the British occupied New York, Sons of Liberty broke into his print shop and left it in ruins. Townsend proved his loyalty to the British not only by writing for the *Gazette* but also by becoming a partner with Rivington in a coffee shop. [3] Gossip in the coffee shop, especially from British officers, gave Townsend many bits of information. One of the officers he got to know was Major John André, the chief British intelligence officer in New York. Rivington flattered André and published his poems. André never realized that both Rivington and Townsend were spying for Washington.

Washington, like any good spymaster, wanted morsels of information from more than one source. While Tallmadge was setting up the Culper Ring, Washington was already getting bits from Nathaniel Sackett, a "Person of Intrigue and Secrecy," who was running his own spy network centered on New York City. Washington knew that Sackett was an experienced spy hunter. He had been on the New York Committee for Detecting and Defeating Conspiracies [4] along with John Jay, president of the Continental Congress and Washington's chief of counterintelligence. [5]

When Sackett switched to running agents for the general, Washington dipped into funds provided by Congress and paid him $50 a month (worth about $800 today) "for your care and trouble in this business" and set aside $500 "to pay those whom you may find necessary to imploy in the transaction of this business."

For Washington, the bits of intelligence he got

from agents were like pieces of a puzzle. These bits of information included where British troops were stationed, what forts were being built, how many warships were entering and leaving New York Harbor, and how much food the troops had.

Washington got the pieces in a roundabout way. Austin Roe, a member of the Culper Ring who ran a tavern in Setauket, often took his wagon into New York City. If a Redcoat sentry stopped him, he would say he was picking up supplies for his tavern. One of his suppliers was Townsend. From Townsend, Roe would get an intelligence report. When Roe returned to Long Island, instead of delivering the

A "DEAD DROP" serves members of Washington's Culper Ring, allowing agents to leave and pick up messages without meeting face to face.

report directly to Abraham Woodhull, he would put it in a box buried on Woodhull's farm. (Modern spies call such a hidden location a dead drop.)

After Woodhull found the report, he would take

out his telescope and check the clothesline of his neighbor, Anna Smith Strong. The British had jailed her husband for "surreptitious correspondence with the enemy." But she bravely carried on as a member of the Culper Ring. If she hung a black petticoat on her clothesline, it meant that another member of the ring, Caleb Brewster, a blacksmith and boatman, had arrived in his boat. The number of white handkerchiefs on the line indicated which of six coves Brewster and his boat were hiding in.

At night, after retrieving the intelligence report, Brewster would sail past British guard boats and cross Long Island Sound to Fairfield, Connecticut. There Brewster kept crews and boats for the cross-sound relay. From Fairfield, a courier on a fast horse would take the report to Tallmadge, who would then hand it to the first of a series of riders stationed 15 miles apart on the route to wherever Washington's headquarters happened to be.

British intelligence officers knew about the Long Island spy traffic. A British report said: "There is one Brewster who has the direction of three Whale Boats that constantly come over from the Connecticut

CLOTHESLINE CODE: Anna Strong hangs her laundry in a way that tells fellow spies the location of the cove where a Culper Ring messenger waits.

Shore once a Week for the purpose of obtaining Intelligence." A British agent in Redding, Connecticut, sent in another report: "Private dispatches are frequently sent" from New York "by way of Setauket, where a certain Brewster receives them, at, or near a certain woman's." Another British spy even had supper with Brewster in Fairfield, but got no worthwhile information.

The man sent by British intelligence to track down Brewster was Nehemiah Marks, a Connecticut man who did for the British what Brewster did for the Americans. Someone, possibly an American officer spying for the British, told Marks enough details about the operation for Marks to be able to seize Brewster, Austin Roe, and two other Patriots working with Roe.

But Marks recommended that the British wait before pouncing on the Americans until he could get even more information. Then Marks would land with a boatload of British agents, go to the place on the coastal road where the first rider picked up the messages from Brewster, and ambush him. Or, as Marks (not a good speller) put it: "Gow & lie in the Cuntry & due thair Best indevore to inter Sept him or thair mails."

For reasons unknown, the ambush never happened. It is an old story to people in the spy game. Many times, then as now, an agent gives his spymaster an idea, and then the spymaster turns it down without saying why.

Washington also got information from agents

he ran himself. One such New York agent was a tailor named Hercules Mulligan. The "fashionable clothier" picked up intelligence tidbits from British officers getting their uniforms fitted in his shop. Washington never revealed Mulligan's achievements, but some historians say the tailor exposed two plots to kill Washington.

Mulligan is believed to have been in contact with an elusive agent named Haym Salomon, a Polish immigrant who spoke German. Unaware that Salomon was a Son of Liberty, the British hired him to translate for officers handling Hessian troops. He passed information to Washington—in a way still unknown—and convinced many Hessians to go over to the American side. Salomon was twice arrested and sentenced to death, but he somehow escaped. Later, in Philadelphia, he used his business talent to raise money for the Revolution.

As intelligence gathering increased and improved, Tallmadge decided that his agents, along with Washington himself, needed secret identities. He took the number 721 and the name John Bolton and passed out other numbers: 722 for Woodhull (Culper Sr.), 723 for Townsend (Culper Jr.), 724 for Austin Roe, 725 for Caleb Brewster, and 711 for George Washington. (You can see the complete code on pages 157–165.)

Some storytellers say there was also a woman, known as Agent 355. But in Tallmadge's codebook "355" means only "lady." The stories say Townsend was in love with Agent 355 and was expecting British counterintelligence officers to arrest them both. According to the stories, only Agent 355 was captured.

✿ ✿

As a spymaster, Washington had to be especially watchful for what he called "double spies." Modern spymasters call them double agents—spies who work for two intelligence services at the same time, giving information to one service about the other. One such double agent was Elijah Hunter, a captain in the American Army. When Hunter showed up at army headquarters, Washington felt that Hunter seemed to be "a sensible man capable of rendering important services," but he knew that it was "necessary to be very circumspect with double spies."

Hunter handed Washington a sample of his ability to swipe intelligence material—a letter that was supposed to go to the commanding officer of British forces in Canada. Washington was suspicious about the letter, wondering if Hunter had been given it by the British and if it was "intended to fall into our Hands." Later, though, when Hunter added solid military intelligence about British units, Washington began to trust him. And Washington, playing his role in the agent's double-dealing, supplied Hunter with such real tidbits as the actual strength of his army and the location of his supply dumps. Washington even suggested that Hunter tell his British case officer that he got the information because American officers "are very incautious in speaking of the strength of their regiments."

Other double agents working for Washington were given the cover of "deserter." He even had them officially listed and denounced for desertion, in case some British agent needed proof that the agent was really a former American soldier and not a spy posing as a deserter. Confused? Even the professionals can get confused. No wonder that a modern spymaster called espionage a "wilderness of mirrors...an ever-fluid landscape where fact and illusion merge."

EXPRESS RIDERS were often Sons of Liberty who, under cover of darkness, carried messages written in code or invisible ink.

Chapter 5.

Tools of the Spymaster.

IN WHICH CODES, *invisible ink, hidden messages, and other devices are put to good use.*

The numbers that Major Tallmadge assigned to members of the Culper Ring were from a secret writing system he invented. He substituted digits for words that would be used in messages. "Long Island," for example, was 728, "arms" was 7, and "city" was 88. There was a number for each month, such as 341 for "January." He made four copies of his codes. He kept one and gave the others to Woodhull, Townsend, and General Washington *(see pages 157–165).* For words that did not have a number code, Tallmadge gave his agents a cipher. In a cipher, each letter in a message is replaced by another letter or a number. When, for example, Abraham Woodhull sent a message to George Washington, this is what the message looked like:

729. 29. 15th 1779

Sir. Dqpeu Beyocpu agreeable to 28. met 723. not far from 727. & received a 356. . . . Every 356. is opened at the entrance of 727. and every 371. is searched, that for the future every 356. must be 691. with the 286. received.

Woodhull didn't bother to encipher (put into code) words such as "Sir" and "from" that would not give away the meaning of the secret message. For "Setauket" and "August" he had code numbers (729 and 29) from his codebook. Washington would translate that first line as "Setauket August 15th 1779." Next, Woodhull has to write a person's name. Because he has no code word for that name, he uses the letter-substitution cipher that Tallmadge had given him:

a b c d e f g h i j k l m n o p q r s t u v w x y z
e f g h i j a b c d o m n p q r k l u v w x y z s t

So a courier named Jonas Hawkins becomes
Dqpeu Beyocpu, and the message reads:

Setauket August 15th 1779

Sir. Jonas Hawkins agreeable to appointment
met Culper Jr. not far from New York &
received a letter . . . Every letter is opened
at the entrance of New York and every man
is searched. that for the future every letter
must be written with the ink received.

Notice that even the deciphered message doesn't
use Robert Townsend's real name; he is always
Culper Jr.

The "ink" that Woodhull mentions is a new kind
of invisible ink that Washington's agents began using
when they didn't want a letter to look like a spy letter. As Washington shrewdly noted, the invisible ink
would not only make "communications less exposed

to detection" but also would "relieve the fears" of agents carrying the innocent-looking messages. Washington knew firsthand the risks of having a letter written in regular ink fall into British hands. It happened to him at least twice.

Both the British and the Americans frequently used horseback riders to carry messages, and both sides tried to capture the riders and get the messages. The rider who lost one of Washington's important messages was Tallmadge himself. It happened when Tallmadge and some of his men were attacked by British troops near the Connecticut–New York border. Tallmadge escaped unharmed but lost a saddlebag full of secret papers.

Luckily, Tallmadge's code did not fall into British hands. But among the papers was a letter from Washington in which he carelessly gave the name and address of an agent, George Higday, saying that he was a man who would probably "convey intelligence to me." Higday was arrested, but he had managed to destroy all evidence of spying. That move probably saved him from hanging.

Another rider, name unknown, lost the other Washington letter, in which the general had written

New Windsor May 29th 1781

Sir,

A day or two ago I requested Col⁰ Harrison to apply to you for a pair of Pincers to fasten the wire of my teeth. I hope you furnished him with them. I now wish you would send me one of your scrapers, as my teeth stand in need of cleaning, and I have little prospect of being in Philadelphia soon. — It will come very safe by the Post — & in return, the money shall be sent so soon as I know the cost of it. —

I am Sir
yr Very hble Serv
G. Washington

WASHINGTON'S LOST LETTER, stolen from a saddlebag by British spies, asks for help from a Philadelphia dentist. Washington wore this denture.

to a dentist in Philadelphia. Washington had suffered from dental problems for many years and eventually had all of his teeth pulled. He wore a denture, made from one of his own teeth, a cow's tooth, and hippopotamus ivory; metal springs held the denture in his mouth. In the letter he asked for "one of your scrapers as my teeth stand in need of cleaning." That information may not sound like much, but a British intelligence officer would get two valuable bits: the name of a pro-American dentist and, even better, from the return address on the letter, the whereabouts of Washington's headquarters.

The idea of invisible ink had been around for a long time. Write using lemon juice as ink, for instance, and the writing will be invisible. Heat the paper, and the writing will appear, looking as if it were written in brown ink. British agents used two types of ink. One could be made visible by holding the paper over the flame of a candle; the other could be read by applying a common chemical. Major John André, the chief British intelligence officer in New York, told his agents to put an F in the corner of letters containing invisible ink needing fire to read and A for those needing acid.

Washington wanted an ink that was more complicated, an ink that could not be read merely by heating the paper or by coating it with an ordinary chemical. And he got what he wanted, from an unexpected source: Sir James Jay, a British doctor who lived in London and dabbled in chemistry.

James Jay, who had been knighted by King George

III, was the brother of a leading Patriot, John Jay. James also did some spying in England. How did he get drawn into the American espionage effort? That is one of many Revolutionary War spy questions that does not yet have an answer.

James Jay's invisible ink did not become visible by heating. As he described it, his ink "would elude the generally known means of detection, and yet could be rendered visible by a suitable counterpart." Jay's invisible ink consisted of two chemicals. An agent used one chemical to write an invisible message. To read the message, the reader had to brush a second chemical on the paper; that chemical made the message visible. The two-bottle system, supplied by

INVISIBLE INK after treatment becomes visible between the lines of a normal letter. To find out who wrote the letter, see Note 1 on page 170.

Jay, gave Washington the secure form of writing that he wanted.

Washington, a spymaster with a sharp eye for details, gave exact instructions on how an agent should use invisible ink: "[H]e should occasionally write his information on the blank leaves of a pamphlet . . . a common pocket book, or on the blank leaves at each end of registers, almanacs, or any new publication or book of small value." He also told his agents that a "much better way" is to write a letter "with some mixture of family matters" and the secret message, which would be invisible, "between the lines and on the remaining part of the sheet."

The British often used a "mask" to keep their messages secret. Hidden within what looked like an ordinary letter was the secret message that was only revealed when the reader applied the mask. The writer might send the letter by one rider going by one route while another rider carried the mask on another route. Such letters had an extra advantage: The writer could include false information in case Americans intercepted the letter.

In the summer of 1777, British General Sir Henry Clinton, in New York City, had to keep in touch with General John Burgoyne, whose troops were heading down the Hudson Valley, and with General Sir William Howe, who was supposed to link up with Burgoyne but instead had chosen to take Philadelphia.

SECRET LETTER: By using a mask (right) General Burgoyne was able to read the secret message in General Clinton's letter (left). Read it for yourself in Note 2 on page 170.

Howe believed that "friends of [the British] Government" along the Hudson would make Burgoyne's task easy. But along the Hudson there were also many enemies of the British. A Peekskill man, for example, although paid to be a courier for Burgoyne, handed the general's message to the Americans. Other British couriers who rode south were never heard from again.

General Clinton, concerned about what General Howe was planning and doing, made use of a mask to write a secret message in a letter to General Burgoyne.

Before writing the letter, Clinton had placed an hourglass-shaped mask on a piece of paper and then had formed the secret message within that shape.

The unmasked letter had enough false information in it to fool any American who happened to see it. But when Burgoyne viewed the letter with the mask, he read Clinton's view of the real situation: Howe has made a bad move; I don't have enough men to do anything about it.

Later, as Clinton's troops were heading up the Hudson Valley, Clinton used another device to pass the news of his whereabouts to Burgoyne. Clinton wrote a message on a piece of silk that he put in a silver ball about the size of a musket ball. (Clinton also sometimes cut a message into long, narrow strips and coiled them into the hollow quill of a large feather.) Clinton gave the silver ball to Daniel Taylor, a young officer, promising that Taylor would be promoted if he got the message to Burgoyne. If he were captured, he was to swallow the ball. Because it was made of silver, it could not harm him.

A SILVER BALL hides a message. If caught, a messenger could swallow the whole thing.

72

Taylor had not gone far before several soldiers in red uniforms stopped him. Believing he was in friendly hands, he said he had a message from "General Clinton." But what he didn't know was that the smiling soldiers were Americans, wearing uniforms swiped from a British ship. They took Taylor to a "General Clinton" who happened to be an American general named George Clinton.

"I am lost!" Taylor cried and swallowed the silver ball. A doctor gave him a strong drug called an emetic, which made him vomit up the ball. Taylor grabbed it and swallowed it again. When General Clinton threatened to kill him and cut his stomach open, Taylor agreed to take another dose of medicine and once again vomited up the ball. The message inside said "...nothing now between us but Gates." This meant that Clinton believed that he, coming from the south, and Burgoyne, coming from the north, were about to trap an American Army led by General Horatio Gates at Saratoga, New York.

But now the Americans knew what was afoot, and they were ready. On September 19, 1777, Redcoats under General Burgoyne clashed with American

WITHIN A FEATHER QUILL General Howe sends an important message to Burgoyne, advising him of his plans. To find out what they are, read Note 3 for this chapter on page 171.

troops, who nearly defeated the British. Burgoyne ordered his men to dig in while awaiting General Clinton's troops, supposedly coming from New York. When no help had come by October 7, Burgoyne launched a desperate attack.

General Gates's troops held their ground. Benedict Arnold, one of Gates's generals, argued for a counterattack that would smash the British force. Gates, outraged that Arnold would challenge his order, took away his command. But the rash Arnold saw a chance to strike a crucial blow. He galloped through the crossfire of both armies, inspiring his men. A bullet struck his leg, but he rode on, leading the final assault that shattered the British fortifications. If he had died of his wounds that day, Arnold would be remembered as one of the great heroes of the Revolutionary War. [4]

Surrounded and outnumbered, Burgoyne finally surrendered on October 17. Meanwhile, Daniel

Taylor had been tried, sentenced to death for espionage, and hanged. When word of the victory at Saratoga reached Taylor's captors, an officer read General Sir Henry Clinton's silk-and-silver secret letter as part of the celebration.

Unknown at the time was the role American agent Alexander Bryan played in the great victory at Saratoga. Bryan was an innkeeper with secret ties to the local Committee of Safety. [5] When General Gates had asked the committee to send him someone who would go behind British lines, Bryan had been picked as "the best qualified to undertake the hazardous enterprise." Leaving behind a sick son and a wife about to have a baby, Bryan boldly entered the British encampment where he learned the size of Burgoyne's force and where he planned to strike the Americans in a surprise attack. [6]

The American victory at Saratoga proved to be a turning point in the war, for it convinced France to come to the aid of America. One agent, Alexander Bryan, had helped to win that battle. And another agent had helped to win France's aid. That agent was Benjamin Franklin.

BENJAMIN FRANKLIN reads a page from his printing press. He served secretly as a Patriot agent in France, in the midst of French and British spies.

Chapter 6.

Franklin's French Friends.

IN WHICH a wise man
from Philadelphia goes to Paris
and outfoxes spies of two nations.

y November 1775 Ben Franklin had become the leading member of the Committee of Secret Correspondence. [1] The committee, created by the Continental Congress, was really a spy agency, set up "for the sole purpose of Corresponding with our friends in Great Britain, Ireland and other parts of the world." France was not mentioned, but France would be the country where Franklin would find America's best friends.

No one else in America had the kind of experience that Franklin brought to the Patriot cause. Well

TWO FOUNDING FATHERS, Benjamin Franklin and George Washington, look over the army in 1775 in Massachusetts. But mostly Franklin worked in France for America.

known as a writer, scientist, and publisher of the *Pennsylvania Gazette*, he had moved to London in 1757 to lobby, first for Pennsylvania and later for Massachusetts and Georgia.

After nearly 17 years in London, he returned home to Philadelphia on May 5, 1775, in the wake of the scandal over the Hutchinson letters. The next day, he was elected to the Continental Congress. His appointment to the Committee of Secret Correspondence led him into a new career in intelligence. He became a partner of spymaster George Washington by serving as a covert operations manager.

He helped on the battlefield by starting a propaganda campaign aimed at Hessians "and other foreigners" hired to fight for the British. Leaflets offering free land to deserters were translated into German and scattered in areas where the Hessians fought. Franklin disguised the leaflets as tobacco packets so the Hessians would be more likely to pick them up. More than 5,000 Hessians deserted during the war, thanks in part to Franklin's propaganda.

George Washington, true to the intelligence rule of keeping bits of espionage in separate boxes, was aware of Franklin's operations but usually did not deal directly with him. This "compartmenting," as modern intelligence officers call it, can sometimes produce problems.

In mid-1775 someone in Bermuda, a British colony off the coast of North Carolina, reported that the royal arsenal at St. George's Island, Bermuda, was full of gunpowder and had no guards around it.

Franklin and Robert Morris, a member of Congress and a money-raiser for the Revolution, arranged for a ship to land some men in Bermuda, grab a ton of gunpowder, and sail to Philadelphia. At the same time, Washington learned about the unguarded gunpowder and asked that a ship of the Rhode Island Navy sail to Bermuda and get the gunpowder. British warships nearly captured the Rhode Island vessel, which returned empty.

Only later did Washington learn that Franklin and Morris had not told him about their operation. Washington must have been angry about the mix-up. But he did not show his anger. Perhaps it was because he really needed the gunpowder or perhaps because he had to stay on friendly terms with Morris, the financial genius of the war. Washington often asked for secret funds from Morris. Once, for instance, Washington requested "hard money," meaning gold or silver, "to pay a certain set of People who are of particular use to us." Morris sent two canvas bags containing "410 Spanish dollars, two English crowns, 10 shillings sixpence, and a French half crown." Obviously, Washington's spies liked to be paid in money that jingled.

❖ ❖ ❖

In December 1775, shortly after Franklin became a member of the Committee of Secret Correspondence, a Frenchman named Julien-Alexander Achard de Bonvouloir, posing as a merchant, arrived in Philadelphia from Europe. His first stop was the home of his friend Francis Daymon, who was teaching Ben Franklin to speak French. The traveler told Daymon that he needed to meet with Franklin on a matter of great importance.

During Franklin's long stay in London he had become well aware of British Secret Service tricks. So when Daymon told him about the stranger, Franklin wondered if he were a British spy. Franklin checked with Washington's counterintelligence expert John Jay, but Jay did not know anything about Bonvouloir. Then Franklin wondered if Bonvouloir might be a French agent, sent to America to get intelligence on the colonists' struggle against England. Since both Franklin and Washington believed that an alliance with France could assure victory in the war, Franklin decided to meet with Bonvouloir.

The Declaration of Independence was still seven months away. American soldiers were dying in an undeclared war with England. The Committee of Safety in New York reported: "We have no arms, we have no powder, we have no blankets." Congress was trying to run a war without having the supplies or the money to do it. And there was no source of supplies or money in sight. France was the best possible source for both.

Franklin's cautious meetings with Bonvouloir led to an addition to George Washington's espionage organization: an overseas intelligence service. Besides running covert operations, including dirty tricks known as sabotage, Franklin's work would include gathering intelligence, sending out counterintelligence agents to hunt for moles and British spies, and using propaganda against England.

For covert operations, Franklin became convinced America needed to have representatives in France. At his urging, Silas Deane, a Connecticut delegate to the Continental Congress, was sent to Paris in 1776 by the Committee of Secret Correspondence. Deane took with him a supply of Sir James Jay's invisible ink. He pretended to be a merchant named Timothy Jones. But he had no training in intelligence, and he didn't fool the British Secret Service, which had a large network in Paris.

Franklin gave Deane a letter of introduction to

HIDDEN BY NIGHT, members of Congress, following separate routes, make their way in the dark to Carpenter's Hall for secret meetings with a French intelligence agent.

Dr. Edward Bancroft, the son of a Connecticut tavern owner who had done some spying for Franklin when he lived in London. Deane didn't really need the letter because Bancroft had been one of his pupils when Deane was a teacher in Hartford, Connecticut. But it was important that it looked like a letter of introduction in case it fell into the wrong hands.

✿ ✿ ✿

Deane at first addressed his reports directly to the Committee of Secret Correspondence. Then

BRITISH SPY Jacobus van Zandt snoops through papers in the desk of American agent Silas Deane in Paris.

someone, probably Franklin, told him to use false addresses in America (today called a "mail drop" or an "accommodation address," where an agent's mail is held for pickup by a case officer). Deane's reports in invisible ink were passed to John Jay, who had the developing chemical that made the writing visible.

Soon after Deane arrived in Paris, he was targeted by a flashy, quick-witted British agent. The agent had lived in New York, and his real name was Jacobus van Zandt. Back in New York he seems to have spied for the British while claiming to be a Son of Liberty. In Paris, he introduced himself as "George Lupton."

Van Zandt reported to the British Secret Service that Deane "strutted about" and acted like "a Child with a new plaything." Van Zandt somehow got Deane out of his apartment long enough to go through Deane's desk. The British agent reported he found nothing of value. Luckily for Deane, van Zandt was soon caught up in a romantic adventure and vanished from Paris, never to spy on Deane again.

Deane, despite his lack of training, managed to set up the most spectacular sabotage operation of the Revolutionary War. A young man who called himself James Aitken (probably not his real name) appeared in Paris out of nowhere and introduced himself to Deane. He said he was an Englishman who had spent time in America and found himself on the side of the Patriots. He told Deane that he had a plan to set fire to England's most important dockyard, at Portsmouth, headquarters of the Royal Navy. Aitken, a house painter also known as "John the Painter," figured that if he could destroy all the rope being made at Portsmouth, the Royal Navy's warships could not sail.

Deane got Aitken a French passport, signed by the French Foreign Minister, and Aitken sailed to England. On December 7, 1776, he set the dockyard on fire, wiping out 20 tons of hemp used to make rope, 6 tons of ordinary rope, and about 6,000 feet of large-size rope. He later burned down two warehouses and several houses in Bristol. The Royal Navy kept on sailing, but the fires panicked England.

Captured in March 1777 after a desperate manhunt, Aitken denied his crimes, but later admitted setting the fires to a British agent posing as a friendly American. He was quickly placed on trial, sentenced to death, and hanged from a 60-foot mast, which, according to a report on the hanging, "was erected at the Main Gate so that he could see the destruction as he passed from this world to the next." His body was placed in a cage that was suspended for months at the dockyard.

Meanwhile, Bonvouloir appeared in Paris and, following Franklin's instructions, contacted Deane. He told Deane to meet secretly with one of the best-known characters in Paris, Pierre Augustin Caron de Beaumarchais. He was not only a friend of King Louis XVI but also an inventor and a writer. Among his writings were plays that would later become famous operas, *The Barber of Seville* and *The Marriage of Figaro*. Beaumarchais had been a spy in Spain, where he had performed some secret missions for the king.

CONVICTED SABOTEUR
"John the Painter" stands in irons outside a prison in England.

When Deane met Bancroft in Paris, he decided to tell Bancroft that he was there to talk to Beaumarchais. The Frenchman had set up a fake firm with a Spanish name (Roderigue Hortalez and Company) to buy and ship guns and other war supplies to America. The company was in fact a screen that shielded the real source of the money: the king of France. (Today, the CIA calls such a shield firm a "proprietary company.")

From French arsenals and other sources Beaumarchais got more than 200 cannon, 25,000 guns, 200,000 pounds of powder, about 20 brass mortars, and shoes, clothing, and tents for 25,000 men. He then found ships to carry the supplies to America. By September 1777 he had shipped supplies that would be worth about half a billion dollars today.

France did not want to openly support America and risk being attacked by Britain. But France wanted to hurt England as payback for the loss of Canada in the French and Indian War. Supplying arms to America meant that Redcoats would be shot by French bullets from French guns—but French soldiers would not have to pull the trigger.

French officials made sure that French markings on the cannon were removed in case the British captured them in battle. But the British, thanks to Bancroft, knew what was going on. (Bancroft also gathered intelligence for Paul Wentworth, a British Secret Service agent who had persuaded Bancroft to spy for the British long before Deane arrived in Paris.) Although he once had been for "the independency of the Colonies," Bancroft decided that he would tell British intelligence "all the information in my power." That turned out to be a lot of information, because Bancroft served as Deane's translator when he met with Beaumarchais. The British gave Bancroft £500 (worth about $38,000 today) and promised him £400 to £500 a year, depending on the outcome of the "American War," as the British called the Revolutionary War. He was also promised a pension of £200 a year.

Bancroft had also been hired by Franklin, who had arrived in Paris to head a three-man commission that would represent the new United States of America in France's royal court. The other two men on the diplomatic commission were Deane and Arthur Lee, who, as a lawyer in London, had spied, at great risk, for the Patriots. [2]

As secretary to the commission, Bancroft would have access to "the progress of the treaty with France," Franklin's correspondence with Congress, and the names and sailing dates of ships that were to "carry war materials"—information that he would pass along to Wentworth.

The British Secret Service gave Bancroft invisible ink and told him how to use it: Write letters to a "Mr. Richards" and sign as "Mr. Edward Edward," with the spy message written between the lines in

DRESSED IN HOMESPUN CLOTHES, Ben Franklin is the
center of attention at a reception held for him by King Louis XVI and his queen.
Franklin was a social star in Paris.

invisible ink. Each Tuesday night after 9:30, Bancroft
was to place the letters in a bottle with a string
attached and put the bottle in a hole near a certain
tree in the Jardin des Tuileries, a beautiful Paris park.
(Spies call this a timed dead drop.) An agent from
the British Embassy ("under diplomatic cover" in
modern spy talk) plucked the bottle out of the hole

and replaced it with another containing instructions to Bancroft. Hundreds of secret commission documents went into and out of the hole.

Franklin and Deane sometimes sent Bancroft on missions to London, not knowing that this gave the double agent a chance to report in person to the head of the British Secret Service. His controllers in England even "arrested" him—but of course he always somehow managed to escape. Arthur Lee became suspicious, but while he was pointing a finger at Bancroft, Franklin learned from his agents in London that Lee's own private secretary was a British spy! To Franklin, Lee was "jealous, suspicious, malignant, and quarrelsome." Lee and Deane argued frequently. First Deane and then Lee was sent back to America. Negotiations with the French continued—and Bancroft kept on spying. [3]

French officials warned the Americans that their most secret information, including word-for-word reports on their conversations with Beaumarchais, were showing up in London within days. A French counterspy had gotten his hands on a British spy's list of ships carrying war supplies from French ports.

Franklin did not seem to be shocked. He may have *wanted* the British to know at least some secrets so that England, fearing that France was close to aiding America, would decide to end the war.

When word of the victory at Saratoga reached France toward the end of 1777, Franklin immediately spread the news. The French reacted "as if it had been a victory of their own troops over their own enemies," the commissioners reported. Both Franklin and the French officials knew that many of the American soldiers who won the battle had fired French bullets from French guns. But officially the French aid was not happening. France still did not want an open alliance with the United States.

Desperate to stop such an alliance, Wentworth begged Franklin to talk to British officials and end the war—on British terms. Franklin probably knew that Wentworth was a British agent and that he was being watched by French counteragents. He told Wentworth not to reveal their conversation, hoping that he would report it to the British. So the meeting played into wise old Franklin's hands. He wanted to hasten an alliance with France. And he knew that the French would see the meeting with Wentworth as a sign that the British might end the war before France officially became involved. Franklin got what he wanted.

The day after the meeting, a French official made the first move toward a French-American alliance. The treaty was signed on February 6, 1778. The signing was a secret, but George III was reading a copy 42 hours later. Franklin had done his job. Now France could officially help America. And America could use all the help it could get.

KING GEORGE III reads a copy of a secret French-American treaty snatched by British spies.

While all these negotiations and undercover activities were going on in Paris, back in America General Washington was facing the loss of Philadelphia, and at the same time the British in New York City seemed to be planning something.

To continue the war with any hope of victory, Washington would have to rely more on his spies than on his soldiers.

AN URGENT MESSAGE is handed to General Washington at a look-out post along the Hudson River north of New York City.

Chapter 7.

Spymaster at Work.

IN WHICH *Washington proves to be a master of deception, and help comes from a surprising source.*

Something was stirring in New York City as the summer of 1777 was ending. Thousands of Redcoats were acting as if they were leaving. Where were they going? Nathaniel Sackett (who you will recall was hand-picked by Washington to run a spy network in New York) found exactly the right agent to get the answer. The British would trust her because she was "the wife of a man gone over to the enemy." Because British food stocks were low, Redcoats had taken grain from her. Sackett told her to go into the city, complain about the loss of her grain, and demand a hearing with General Sir William Howe, commander of British forces. Meanwhile, she was to pick up all the information she could and then make her way back to Sackett, who was in Westchester County, just outside New York.

We do not know the agent's name, and we do not know if she got a hearing before Howe. But, from a report Sackett later wrote, we know the most important facts she learned: The British were building many flat-bottomed boats and were planning to invade Philadelphia and "subdue that city." [1]

Washington could slow down Howe, but his ragged army had little chance of keeping the British from sending troops from New York to occupy Philadelphia. Outnumbered nearly two to one, Washington's army had 7,000 men—about 1,000 of them without shoes. Philadelphia, where the Continental Congress had created a new nation by drafting and signing the Declaration of Independence in July 1776, was doomed. Congressmen fled to York, Pennsylvania. On September 26, 1777, the British, under Howe, marched into Philadelphia.

Washington made camp at Whitemarsh, about 12

miles northwest of Philadelphia, and planned his next move. Thanks to the advance work of Sackett and his woman agent, Washington already had a spy network set up in Philadelphia. Some agents he ran personally; some worked under Major John Clark, a brilliant Continental Army officer "on spy service."

STRIKING A BLOW FOR LIBERTY, a Patriot knocks down the royal coat of arms from a building in Philadelphia.

Our information on what was happening in and around Philadelphia comes from Washington's reports, letters, and diaries and from family stories handed down generation to generation. Just as Washington himself had to put the whole intelligence and counterintelligence picture together from bits of information, so must we. Piecing our bits together, we get a picture of the Philadelphia spy story.

One of the key pieces of the story is Washington's use of deception. He seemed to enjoy fooling the British, right from the beginning. Soon after taking command of the Continental Army in July 1775, for example, he learned that his soldiers had only 36 barrels of gunpowder—about nine shots for each man. He sent agents into British-occupied Boston with the story that his army had *1,800* barrels. And, to raise morale, he had the same reports planted among his own men.

Several times during the war Washington arranged for fake documents to fall into the hands of known British spies. He set up the deception so that British scouts stopped his horseback couriers and grabbed the fake documents, thinking they were real. Or he had British riders stopped and their saddlebags examined. The contents of the saddlebags were then returned—along with documents that had been created by Washington's men but that looked like real British documents. (Spies are often good counterfeiters.)

One of the most complicated deceptions Washington ever put together came after Howe occupied Philadelphia. Washington knew that his men in Whitemarsh would be overwhelmed if the British sent troops from both New York and Philadelphia. But Washington also knew that Gates's victory over the British at Saratoga, less than a month after the British occupied Philadelphia, worried Howe and Clinton (now in charge of British troops in New York), for they had no idea where Gates would strike next.

Washington wanted Howe to think that Gates's army was heading for Philadelphia, which meant Howe had to keep his Redcoats in that city. And, to keep the British pinned down in New York City, Washington wanted Clinton to think that Gates's troops were on their way there. (In fact, Gates was not sure what to do and did not go to either city.)

As part of the deception, Washington ordered three generals with troops near New York to act as if they were preparing to invade the city. They were also told to make sure that their "secret" moves became known to "persons who you are sure will divulge" those secrets. Those persons were New York Tories who were being fed false information ("disinformation" in spy talk) by American counter-intelligence agents.

For the Philadelphia part of the deception, Washington brought in Major Clark and told him to have one of his agents appear to become a traitor. Among his agents Clark found one who agreed to go to Howe and offer to "risque my all in procuring him intelligence." Howe, cautious about dealing with a traitor, asked to see what the man had to offer. He brought Howe a stack of documents—some written by Washington just for the deception. Among them was a paper showing that Gates was sending 8,000 men to help Washington capture Philadelphia. Howe fell for the deception long enough for Washington to dig in at Whitemarsh and for Major Clark to train his agents.

Major Clark, as director of the most important Philadelphia spy network, gave many of his agents

TEUCRO DUCE NIL DESPERANDUM.

First Battalion of PENNSYLVANIA LOYALISTS, commanded by His Excellency Sir WILLIAM HOWE, K.B.

ALL INTREPID ABLE-BODIED

HEROES,

WHO are willing to serve His MAJESTY KING GEORGE the Third, in Defence of their Country, Laws and Constitution, against the arbitrary Usurpations of a tyrannical Congress, have now not only an Opportunity of manifesting their Spirit, by assisting in reducing to Obedience their too-long deluded Countrymen, but also of acquiring the polite Accomplishments of a Soldier, by serving only two Years, or during the present Rebellion in America.

Such spirited Fellows, who are willing to engage, will be rewarded at the End of the War, besides their Laurels, with 50 Acres of Land, where every gallant Hero may retire, and enjoy his Bottle and Lass.

Each Volunteer will receive, as a Bounty, FIVE DOLLARS, besides Arms, Cloathing and Accoutrements, and every other Requisite proper to accommodate a Gentleman Soldier, by applying to Lieutenant Colonel ALLEN, or at Captain KEARNY's Rendezvous, at PATRICK TONRY's, three Doors above Market-street, in Second-street.

RECRUITMENT POSTER urges pro-British colonists to join a Loyalist regiment. (Colonel Allen is not an ancestor of the author.)

the cover of farmer or merchant. The British allowed these people to pass in and out of Philadelphia because they were helping to feed the city. Other agents moved in and out under the cover of smugglers. They were allowed to pass because they could supply British officers with scarce goods. The comings and goings of all these "privileged" Philadelphians violated Washington's strict order against allowing such travel, but of course, his counterintelligence officers ignored the order so the "proper persons" could get their reports to Clark.

Legend says that some agents did not take their information directly to the American encampment at Whitemarsh but instead passed it on to a woman known as "Old Mom" Rinker. She was said to have a unique way of getting the information to the next stop on the spy underground. She bleached her flax on a rock atop a cliff in the Wissahickon Valley in Germantown, which is now part of Philadelphia. Nearby was her family's inn, Buck's Tavern, where Washington once set up overnight headquarters. She often sat by her rock, knitting.

A Patriot guerrilla force called the Green Boys

watched over the area—and at least once ambushed a Hessian patrol. The Green Boys kept an eye on Old Mom, and when she "accidentally" dropped a ball of yarn over the cliff, they watched where it landed. After quietly retrieving it, they unrolled the yarn, removed the agent messages hidden inside, and took them to Washington's headquarters. [2]

Washington's deceptions kept Howe from attacking for a while, but deceptions cannot last forever. In November 1777 Howe began planning a battle that would defeat Washington so thoroughly that he would be forced to surrender, and the Revolutionary War would end in a major British victory. In Washington's words, a strong attack by Howe "might prove the ruin of our cause."

Howe's plan was upset not by one of Major Clark's agents but by a woman who became a spy on her own.

✿ ✿
✿

Lydia Darragh and her family were living on Second Street in Philadelphia when British troops entered the city in September 1777. The mother of four, she worked as a nurse, a midwife, and even as an undertaker to help support her family. Her husband, William, was a teacher. A strong, wise woman 48 years old, she had come to America from Dublin, Ireland. She was a Quaker, as members of the Society of Friends were called. As such, she was believed to be against the war.

She had seen a neighboring family put out of their house when General Howe decided to set up his headquarters there. So she was not surprised when Major John André, an officer on Howe's staff, ordered the Darragh family out of their home. It was needed, he said, for British officers. She protested, saying she still had two children at home.

Lydia decided to go to Howe and ask that her house not be

KNITTING A PLOT. "Old Mom" Rinker drops her ball of yarn over a cliff; fellow spies pluck the ball, which has important messages from spies in Philadelphia.

taken. According to one story, at Howe's headquarters she spotted a British officer who was a second cousin from Ireland. He helped her talk Howe into letting her stay in her home as long as she would let British officers use her large living room (then called a parlor) for meetings.

Lydia Darragh's career as a secret agent is not easy to track. Most information about her work comes down to us from her daughter, Ann. At some point, apparently as a lone volunteer without training, Lydia decided to snoop around. She sent whatever she and other family members learned to her son Lieutenant Charles Darragh, who was in Washington's army at Whitemarsh.

Her husband first wrote the information in a kind of family code, or shorthand. Lydia put the tiny pieces of paper inside cloth-covered buttons. She then sewed the buttons on the coat of her 14-year-old son, John. An expert at getting through British lines, John made his way to Charles. John then cut off his buttons and handed them to Charles, who took out the bits of paper and translated the shorthand messages for intelligence officers. We know now what Lydia did, but we still do not know what was in those tiny reports.

On December 2, 1777, Major André told Lydia

that he needed to use her parlor that night. All the family was to go to bed early so that no one would be around when the officers met. The British arrived around eight o'clock. Sensing that this was an important meeting, Lydia tiptoed to the locked door and listened. (Another version has her hiding in a closet to eavesdrop.) She heard Howe's top officers discussing what sounded like a plan for a surprise attack on Washington's army. Finally, she heard an officer reading the actual order for British troops to march from the city at dawn on December 4 and head for Whitemarsh.

She slipped into her bedroom and made believe she was sleeping. After the meeting, André knocked on her door repeatedly until she sleepily answered. Convinced that she had not been wandering around during the secret conference, André went on his way.

Meanwhile, in the first days of December intelligence reports about British troop movements began streaming into Washington's headquarters from various sources. On December 3 Major Clark gave Washington information only hours old: "This morning, a Sergeant, a countryman of my spy's, assured him that the Troops had received orders to hold themselves in readiness when called for, and to draw two days provisions. Biscuit was served out to them when he came away, and 'twas the current language in the city among the Troops and citizens that they were going to make a move."

LYDIA DARRAGH tells an American officer what she heard while eavesdropping on a British meeting in her home.

Another source was Elias Boudinot, a delegate from New Jersey to the Continental Congress who went into the army as a colonel and became superintendent of British prisoners of war. That may not sound like the job of an intelligence officer, but Boudinot could get information from his prisoners—deliberately or accidentally. And, as Washington later remarked, Boudinot had "better opportunities than most other officers in the army, to obtain knowledge of the Enemy's Situation, motions and...designs."

Washington left to our imagination exactly how Boudinot must have spied on prisoners. He probably eavesdropped on their conversations or perhaps he "turned" some so they would betray their comrades in exchange for extra privileges. Whatever Boudinot's duties as supervisor of prisoners, he was certainly working in intelligence on December 3, when Lydia left her house, went to Howe's headquarters, and asked her cousin for a pass so that she could go to a flour mill outside the city.

Family legend has her trudging through the snow, carrying an empty flour sack. According to her daughter, Ann, shortly before Lydia reached the Rising Sun Tavern, north of Philadelphia, she met a member of the Pennsylvania militia and told him what she had heard the night before. He said he would take her report immediately to Washington.

Long after the war, Boudinot told another story. He said that on December 3 he was in the Rising Sun Tavern, not far from the flour mill, collecting intelligence from Philadelphia agents. A "little poor-looking insignificant Old Woman came in & solicited leave to go into the Country to buy some flour," he later wrote. "While we were asking some Questions, she walked up to me and put into my hands a dirty old needle book, with various small pockets in it." She then left the tavern.

Boudinot searched through the book and "found a piece of paper rolled up....On unrolling it I found information that General Howe was coming out the next morning with 5,000 men, 13 pieces of cannon, baggage wagons, and 11 boats on wheels. On comparing this with other information, I found it true and immediately rode post to headquarters."

What is the real story? We will never know. Whatever the details, *some* woman gave Washington vital information. And we also know that the Rising Sun Tavern for a while was a spy nest. Besides appearing in the Darragh and Boudinot stories, the tavern and another volunteer woman agent both found their way into a journal written by Benjamin Tallmadge, Washington's intelligence chief.

Tallmadge tells about "a country girl," sent into Philadelphia supposedly to sell eggs but told to "obtain some information respecting the enemy." Tallmadge was "at a tavern called the Rising Sun,"

TO THE RESCUE! Major Benjamin Tallmadge, Washington's intelligence chief, saves a "country girl"—a spy—from British pursuers.

getting a report from the egg seller when he was warned that British cavalry were nearby. "Stepping to the door," he wrote, "I saw them at full speed chasing in my patrols." Tallmadge leaped to his saddle, hoisted up the woman, and galloped off. During a three-mile ride, "although there was considerable firing of pistols, and not a little wheeling and charging, she remained unmoved, and never once complained of fear."

From countless trained and volunteer sources, including perhaps Lydia Darragh, Old Mom, and the egg seller, Washington got enough information to spoil the British plan. By strengthening his forces at the places where he knew that Howe was about to attack, the master of deception made it look as though reinforcements had arrived. Howe, believing reports that Washington had 4,000 additional troops, did not launch a major attack. He took his troops back to Philadelphia.

Howe's intelligence officers firmly believed that someone had passed the British plan to Washington. According to Ann Darragh, Major André returned to the Darragh home and asked Lydia whether everyone had been asleep on the night of December 2. She convinced him that everyone had gone to bed early, and André left, saying, "One thing is certain—the enemy had notice of our coming, were prepared for us, and we marched back like a parcel of fools. The walls must have ears." [3]

Things stayed fairly quiet in Philadelphia until May, when General Sir Henry Clinton took over command of Philadelphia from General Howe.

When Clinton learned that French troops had begun arriving in America, he realized he must return to New York. Suddenly, British customers were giving the laundries in Philadelphia rush orders to deliver clothing "finished or unfinished." Women agents who worked in the laundries passed the word. This is how Washington learned that the British were about to speedily depart. [4]

One of the officers who left Philadelphia when the British pulled out of the city in June 1778 was Major André. He would continue his job as a British spymaster by running agents in New York, including Ann Bates, a former Philadelphia schoolteacher who had left that city at the same time as the British. Sent into Washington's camp disguised as a peddler, she would bring back solid reports on the number of cannon and the number of Continental troops, regiment by regiment.

Washington put General Benedict Arnold in command of the American forces that entered Philadelphia after the British left. It would not be long before Major John André and General Benedict Arnold would meet.

CATCHING A BRITISH SPY, militiamen grab Major John André, who carries plans for the defense of West Point, given to him by an American traitor.

Chapter 8.

The General
Is a Spy.

IN WHICH a traitor
offers to sell out his country
for British gold.

Some time after General Benedict Arnold took command in Philadelphia, he sent for Joseph Stansbury, a local merchant who was despised by Patriots. Why, Philadelphians wondered, would Arnold want to have anything to do with Stansbury? He was a hated Tory. Before the British occupied the city, Stansbury taunted Patriots by singing "God Save the King," urging them to join him in the chorus. He was arrested for his Tory activities and briefly jailed. When the Redcoats marched into Philadelphia, the Patriots despised Stansbury even more, because he went to work for the British, doing various jobs for General Howe.

To Stansbury's surprise, he later wrote, Arnold "communicated to me, under a solemn obligation of secrecy, his intention of opening his services to the commander-in-chief of the British forces...." In other words, Arnold wanted to be a double agent for the British. [1]

Arnold a spy for the British? Stansbury could hardly believe it. Arnold was a brave and faithful soldier. He had run away from home at the age of 14 to fight in the French and Indian War. He had joined the Continental Army as a colonel and had led soldiers to victories at Fort Ticonderoga and at Saratoga. He had twice been wounded in battles against the British. Washington considered Arnold to be his finest battlefield commander.

Limping from his wounds, Arnold could not hold a field command. So Washington had put him in charge of American forces in Philadelphia. Arnold lived grandly, holding parties and spending money far beyond his soldier pay. Arnold needed money to live in a mansion and keep his stylish new bride happy. She was the beautiful 19-year-old Peggy Shippen. The daughter of a wealthy Tory family, she was also a close friend of Major John André, England's chief of intelligence in America. Complaints from Congress about Arnold piled up. A military court found that his greed for money and power had led to his involvement in shady deals.

After meeting with Arnold, Stansbury later wrote, "I went secretly to New York" and contacted André.

André used Stansbury as a "cut-out," a person who links the agent and the case officer. By using a cut-out, André could stay in New York and never be caught in the company of his agent.

PEGGY ARNOLD, wife of Benedict Arnold, posed for this portrait by her friend British intelligence officer John André.

André, through Stansbury, taught Arnold to write in invisible ink and to use a "book code," a tough code to break. The code was based on a well-known book owned by both André and Arnold: Blackstone's *Commentaries on the Laws of England.* As André explained the code,

"Three Numbers make a Word." The first number is the page of the book, the second is the line on that page, and the third is the word on that line, counting from the left. *293.9.7,* for example, directs André to page 293, line 9, word 7.

Not every word was put into numbers. That was a tricky part of the code. If someone happened to see a letter written by Arnold or André, it would look like the kind of coded letter that merchants would normally write to keep their business secrets from being learned by competitors. For instance, Arnold would not write out Stansbury's name. He would just write Mr. S and André would fill in the rest. Here is part of a letter from Arnold to André:

> I 293.9.7 to C___t. B. 103.8.2. the 7th 152.9.17.
> that , a F___ 112.9.17. and 22.8.29 were 105.9.50
> to 4 9.71 in 62.8.20 with, 163.8.19 A 22.8.19 at
> with 230.8.13.   263.8.17 I gave Mr. S---y a
> 164.8.16 147.8.261 to be 209.9.216 in C----a

André, using his copy of the book, would decode the numbers. In the decoded version, letters inside brackets show how André would finish the words where only the first letter had been given:

> I wrote to Captn B[eckwith]-on the 7th of June, that a F[rench]--- fleet and army were expected to act in conjunction with the A[merican]--- army. At the same time I gave Mr. S[tansbur]y a manifesto intended to be published in C[anad]----a

Arnold passed the British many secrets, such as how many French troops were landing in America and where and when they were landing. He also revealed an American-French deception plan (the "manifesto" mentioned in the letter) that was supposed to make the British expect an invasion of Canada. But, when Arnold told them that he was to take command of the fort at West Point, the British knew they had a man who could give them the most important military post in America.

West Point guarded the Hudson River, a prize that the Americans held and the British desperately wanted. British generals saw West Point as a key to

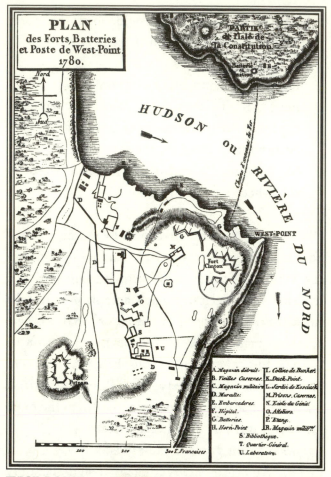

PLAN
des Forts, Batteries
et Poste de West-Point.
1780.

Nord

Sud

HUDSON ou RIVIÈRE DU NORD

PARTIE de l'Isle de la Constitution

Batterie

Chaîne à travers le Fer

WEST-POINT

Fort Clinton

Fort Putnam

A. *Magasin détruit.*	I. *Colline de Bunker.*
B. *Vieilles Casernes.*	K. *Duck-Point.*
C. *Magasin militaire.*	L. *Jardin de Kosciusk.*
D. *Muraille.*	M. *Prisons. Casernes.*
E. *Embarcaderes.*	N. *Ecole du Génie.*
F. *Hôpital.*	O. *Ateliers.*
G. *Batteries.*	P. *Etang.*
H. *Horn-Point.*	R. *Magasin militre.*

S. *Bibliotheque.*
T. *Quartier-Général.*
U. *Laboratoire.*

100   300   500 T. Francaises

WEST POINT, guardian of the Hudson River. This French map shows the great chain that blocked the Royal Navy from the upper Hudson.

victory. A glance at a military map shows why. The fortress stood on a high bluff on a sharp curve of the river about 50 miles north of New York City. From its heights, West Point looked down on smaller forts on both sides of the river. Stretched across the Hudson was an enormous iron chain that blocked enemy warships. As long as the West Point complex of forts was held by the Americans, its guns would keep enemy ships from ascending the river. If the British held West Point, they could cut off the northeastern colonies from the others.

SECRET CODE hides Benedict Arnold's message to Major John André about West Point. To find out where you can read a decoded version of the letter, see Note 2 on page 172.

Washington had hoped that Arnold would be able to take command of combat troops. But Arnold, claiming that his old wounds still kept him from battle duty, successfully pleaded for command of West Point. As soon as he got the post, he offered to arrange the surrender of West Point to the British for £20,000, a sum equal to well over one million dollars today.

Anxious to make the deal, Arnold insisted on a personal meeting with André—a very dangerous move, especially for the case officer. Such a move has to be arranged in a complicated way, with cutouts, coded letters, and a "safe house," a place where the case officer and his agent will not be detected by counterspies. Each step along the way is risky, because the enemy's counterintelligence officers often notice some little slip that leads to capture.

Washington learned from some of his agents operating in New York that "some secret expedition is in contemplation, the success of which depends altogether on its being kept a secret." That bit of information did not help very much—until afterward, when Washington and others realized that the "secret expedition" was the seizing of West Point by the British as soon as Arnold betrayed it.

Arnold tried to learn the identities of American agents in New York by writing first to Washington and then to one of his officers. Neither one would help him because of a basic spy law: Give information only to those with a need to know. Arnold was not one of those people.

Major Benjamin Tallmadge, who was running New York's Culper Ring, heard about Arnold's inquiries. He certainly must have become suspicious, especially when he got a letter from Arnold saying that a Mr. John Anderson, "a person I expect from New York," should be given an escort and taken to Arnold. Tallmadge had to wonder why Arnold was running his own agent in New York.

Meanwhile, Arnold arranged for a boat, under a flag of truce, to take a Tory woman and her children across the Hudson to an area held by the British. The woman carried a letter to André, asking him to come to West Point disguised as a merchant named John Anderson. André refused, for he was well aware that if he disguised himself, he could be hanged as a spy; if he was captured in uniform, he would live as a prisoner of war.

Arnold insisted that he could protect André, claiming him as an agent working for the Americans. Finally, André reluctantly agreed to wear civilian clothes. Arnold arranged to meet André at a safe house on the Hudson River. But British gunboats fired on the barge that was carrying Arnold across the river, and he was forced to return to West Point.

For the next meeting, André, dressed in the uniform of a British officer, was to arrive via a British warship, the *Vulture*. He would be dropped off downriver from West Point. There, a Tory friend of Arnold would pick up André and take him to Arnold. The general's cover story was that André was really an agent named John Anderson whom Arnold was personally running. André did not like the cover story, but he went along with the plan.

As Arnold and André were meeting at a riverside safe house, they heard gunfire. American cannon were firing on the *Vulture*, which quickly weighed anchor and sailed away. André now had no exit.

Arnold had brought sketches of the fortifications of West Point, which André, as an experienced intelligence officer, memorized and handed back to Arnold. But the general, to ensure he would get paid the money that had been promised him, insisted that André take the sketches as proof that Arnold had carried out his side of the bargain. Reluctantly, André

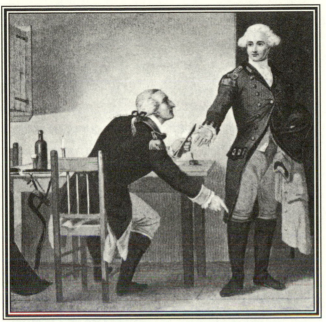

PLOTTING TREASON. Benedict Arnold points to John André's boots, where André will hide the West Point plans that Arnold is going to give him.

put the sketches inside his boots. He hastily disguised himself by replacing his red coat with a purple one and putting on a round civilian hat. His boots had no military markings and could pass as civilian.

Arnold assured André that he would be safe going overland to the British lines because he would have a pass signed by General Arnold himself. While the general made his way back to West Point, André set off for White Plains, New York. There the pass supposedly would get him through American lines to safety in British-held territory.

But three American militiamen stopped him on the road. In the darkness he thought at first they were Hessians or British and identified himself as a British officer. Then, seeing that the men were Americans, he shrugged that off as a joke. When they said they would search him, he tried to bribe them with his gold watch and the equivalent of $50,000.

"I searched his person effectually, but found nothing until I pulled off his boot, when we discovered that something was concealed in his stocking," one of the militiamen later wrote. "... I pulled off his stocking, and inside of it, next to the sole of his foot, found three half sheets of paper enclosed in another half sheet which was endorsed 'West Point;' and on pulling off the other boot and stocking, I found three like paper...."

The militiamen took him to an American outpost, where, thanks to an order from Arnold, "Mr.

Anderson" was expected. The officer at the outpost sent the "suspicious papers" to Washington—who never received them—and sent Anderson, under guard, to Arnold. This was good news to André.

That night, Major Tallmadge happened to be at another nearby American outpost. There he learned that someone named Anderson had been picked up and sent on to General Arnold. Tallmadge, remembering the "Anderson" order from Arnold, felt that Anderson and Arnold were plotting something. Tallmadge ordered Anderson brought to him. The outpost officer, who outranked Tallmadge, reluctantly agreed but insisted that a report about Anderson be sent on to Arnold at West Point—where Arnold was expecting a visit from George Washington.

André, under questioning by Tallmadge, drew on his talents as an amateur actor and posed as a misunderstood merchant. But the sharp-eyed Tallmadge knew from the way that André paced across the floor that he had to be a military officer. André finally admitted his identity, but insisted he was a combat officer, not a spy. Tallmadge instantly realized that Arnold was a traitor.

FLEEING FOR HIS LIFE. Arnold heads for a boat that will take him to a Royal Navy warship. If caught, he faces hanging for treason.

Arnold got the report on the capture of Anderson and the "suspicious papers" before Washington arrived. He knew immediately he had been unmasked. He ran out of the room, rode a horse to the riverside, and ordered his bargemen to take him downriver to the *Vulture*. When they looked at him suspiciously, he said that he had to meet with the warship's captain because of "particular business from

Washington." As soon as the barge reached the warship, Arnold climbed aboard and had the bargemen arrested as prisoners of war.

When Washington arrived at West Point, he learned of Arnold's treachery. "Great Arnold has stolen off to the enemy!" he is said to have exclaimed. He ordered Captain Alexander Hamilton to lead a search for Arnold. Then, according to a witness, Washington left the room and, "giving way to an uncontrollable burst of feeling," wept. This was the first time anyone had ever seen Washington cry.

Early the next day, Tallmadge took André to Washington's headquarters at Tappan, New York. There he was put on trial before a military court, which found him guilty.

In a message sent under a flag of truce, Washington told British General Henry Clinton, in New York, that he would spare André's life if Clinton turned over Arnold. Clinton would not allow the exchange. Arnold wrote Washington and threatened that if André were hanged, Arnold would "retaliate on such unhappy Persons of your Army as may fall within my Power." Washington ordered André hanged. [3] With Tallmadge standing nearby, André was hanged in full-dress uniform. His last words were, "I pray you bear me witness that I met my fate like a brave man."

Arnold, safe in British-occupied New York, was commissioned as a British brigadier general. He immediately started looking for American spies in New York. He flushed out Hercules Mulligan and ordered him arrested, but Mulligan outwitted Arnold and was released. An unproved story has persisted that Arnold had Agent 355 held captive aboard the prison ship *Jersey*, anchored off Brooklyn, and that she was one of thousands of prisoners who died on that hulk of horror.

Washington ordered Major "Light Horse Harry" Lee to take charge of what today would be called a special operation: the kidnapping of Benedict Arnold. For the operation, Lee picked his sergeant major, John Champe, a man "full of bone and muscle" and "tried courage." Champe was "charmed with the plan," which Washington himself had hatched: Pretend you are a deserter. Slip into British-held New York City. Kidnap Arnold. Get him to waiting agents in New Jersey. And do not harm him. He must be publicly hanged.

Champe "stole" some official papers from Lee as part of his cover, hopped on a horse, and headed for New York. Lee told no one about the mission that Washington had entrusted to Champe. So Champe was on his own when he tried to get through American lines then make his way through British lines to get into New York City.

Lee thought all was going well until one of his officers rushed up to him and reported that a patrol had ordered an American to stop. The man "put spur to his horse and escaped"—but not for long. The patrol spotted him again and chased him until he neared the Hudson River. There, he jumped off his horse, leaped into the water, and swam toward a British patrol boat, yelling for help. The British fired at Champe's pursuers and took him aboard.

The British, impressed by the deserter's bravery, took him before General Henry Clinton. Clinton sent him to Arnold, who had formed an "American Legion" of Tories and deserters. As soon as he joined the legion, Champe took note of Arnold's habits and,

AMERICAN SPY John Champe swims to a welcoming British patrol boat after out-running pursuing Americans, who think he is a deserter.

with the aid of two of Washington's agents in New York, plotted a kidnapping.

Sergeant Champe got word of the plan to Lee. On the night the kidnapping was to happen, Lee led a patrol to the New Jersey side of the Hudson and waited with three extra horses—"one for Arnold, one for the sergeant, and the third for his [Champe's] associate," Lee later wrote. "Hour after hour passed, no boat approached." [4] The kidnap plot failed because on the night it was to happen Arnold loaded his American Legion, including Champe, on board a transport and sailed to Virginia, where he attacked Richmond. Champe became a deserter again—this time a real deserter—and found his way to Washington. Fearing that Champe would be executed if Arnold caught him, Washington discharged him from the Continental Army.

The next would-be Arnold kidnapper was an experienced agent named Allan McLane. (He once had disguised himself as a simple country yokel and prowled a British fort for two weeks.) Captain McLane felt sure that he could kidnap Arnold when the general took his morning ride along Chesapeake Bay. But McLane also failed because, at the last minute, British warships unexpectedly appeared. Thomas Jefferson, governor of Virginia, was the next plotter. He concocted a scheme to abduct "this greatest of traitors" while he was leading raids in Virginia. Once again, Arnold was too well guarded. He continued his career as a British officer until the end of the war, when he sailed to England. [5]

WASHINGTON FIRES THE FIRST SHOT at Yorktown. His
deception plan led to victory in the Revolution, a war of shooting—and spying.

Chapter 9.

Victory in the Spy War.

IN WHICH *the spymaster
leads the British into a final trap
and wins the war.*

George Washington was fighting a war with a visible army and an invisible army. Even when the visible army was being beaten on battlefields, Washington's invisible army was winning victories in the back alleys of the spy war. By stealing and reading secret messages and by reading the decoded reports of agents and spy hunters, Washington was finding out what the British were going to do sometimes even before British troops knew. All the while, Washington the general was using the discoveries of Washington the spymaster to move toward the moment when he could hurl his army into a battle that would decide the war.

That moment came in 1781, thanks to two weapons of the invisible army: deception and the Culper Ring.

✻ ✻ ✻

By 1780 General Sir Henry Clinton, successor to General Howe as commander of the British forces in America, had split his troops in two. Some were in New York City, which remained the capital of wartime British America; the rest, including Arnold's American Legion, were in the South. After the Redcoats swept through Georgia and South Carolina, Clinton put General Charles Cornwallis in command of all troops in the South.

Clinton had been expecting a battle against an American-French force ever since 1778, when France had decided to aid the Americans. One of Clinton's agents in Connecticut had predicted what would happen next: "an attack upon New York & Long Island is designed as soon as the French Troops arrive, in conjunction with the Continental Troops—Mr. Washington is to have the Chief Command over the whole."

British agents in France and America had supplied Clinton with all the details about the French expedition long before a fleet of French warships, carrying about 7,600 soldiers, arrived at Newport, Rhode Island, on July 10, 1780. Clinton planned to strike the French before Washington even knew about the landing. On July 11 Washington told his chief of intelligence, Major Benjamin Tallmadge, "As we may every moment expect the arrival of the French fleet, a revival of the correspondence with the Culpers will be of a very great importance." British intelligence, with its thorough knowledge of the French landing, was ahead of the Culpers. America was behind in the intelligence war.

THE FRENCH ARRIVE in Rhode Island, beginning a series of moves that will fool the British into expecting an American-French attack on New York.

Tallmadge contacted Townsend (Culper Jr.) and told him to put together as much information about British activities as he could gather from his

RELAY RACE by Culper spy ring delivers "news of the greatest consequence" from Townsend to Roe to Woodhull to Brewster to Washington.

sources in New York City. Townsend then wrote all that he learned in invisible ink between the lines of an ordinary-looking message and got it to Austin Roe, the Setauket tavern owner. Roe passed it to Abraham Woodhull (Culper Sr.). Using one of the Culper Ring's secret relay operations, Woodhull gave it to Caleb Brewster, the boatman, with an additional message addressed to Brewster: "Sir. The enclosed requires your immediate departure this day by all means let not an hour pass; for this day must not be lost. You have news of the greatest consequence perhaps that ever happened to your country."

On July 21, in the Culper Ring's quickest agent-to-spymaster delivery, the intelligence gathered by Townsend reached Washington at Dobbs Ferry on the Hudson River, about 20 miles north of New York City. Townsend had discovered that about 8,000 Redcoats were boarding ships to sail to Newport, where they would launch an attack on the French troops. Washington did not have enough soldiers or time to stop the British from sailing to Newport. So he reached for his favorite intelligence weapon: deception.

He hastily put together a plan that would convince Clinton that 12,000 American soldiers were about to pounce on New York City. The plan, full of details intended to fool Clinton, was put into a pouch and given to an agent pretending to be a Tory farmer. He gave it to a British intelligence officer, telling him that he had found the pouch lying on the road.

Clinton panicked. Knowing that he would need

the fleet to help defend the city, he decided to call back the ships, which had set off for Newport under full sail. Signal fires flared along Long Island's north shore. The signals were orders to the ships' captains: Turn the fleet back to New York. Washington's deception had worked. He had saved the French fleet from attack.

Nearly a year later, Washington and Count Jean B. de Rochambeau, the general commanding the French troops, began planning a real attack on New York. The plan was based on the belief that Admiral François de Grasse's powerful French fleet, with 3,000 troops, was heading from France to New York to aid in the attack. Then in August 1781 came a report that de Grasse had decided instead to sail to Chesapeake Bay to fight British forces in Virginia. Washington and Rochambeau rapidly changed their plan: They would head south to Virginia with the goal of trapping Cornwallis's troops gathering at Yorktown, near the mouth of Chesapeake Bay.

Meanwhile, reports about a looming Washington-Rochambeau attack on New York City spread through Clinton's spy network. One of Clinton's best agents, David Gray, provided him with many details about the preparations for an attack. What Clinton did not know was that Gray was a double agent whose information came directly from Washington. The spymaster knew from his own network that Clinton already had much of the intelligence anyway. So Washington decided to give Gray even more bits of truth to ensure that Gray would be trusted by his British handlers.

British agents sent numerous reports to their case officers, tracking the French as they set out from Rhode Island to join up with the Americans. The deception plan called for the French and American armies to *seem* to be forming for an attack on New York. The real plan was for the two armies to link up in New York but then actually head south to Virginia.

A FALSE MESSAGE carried by an American courier hoodwinks the British.

The British captured an American courier and found documents (deliberately planted) that added to Clinton's belief that New York was the American-French target. Clinton ordered General Cornwallis in Virginia to send reinforcements to New York, a move that weakened Cornwallis's force.

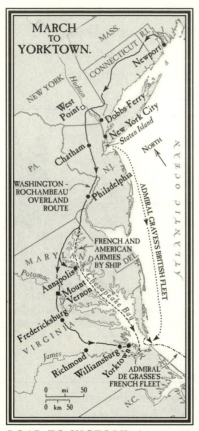

MARCH TO YORKTOWN.

ROAD TO VICTORY. American and French soldiers travel to Yorktown, where French warships close the trap on British troops.

For a while, even American troops believed they were going to attack New York. Officers ordered them to clear and repair roads to the city. One regiment in New Jersey marched toward Staten Island. "If we do not deceive our own men," Washington later wrote, "we will never deceive the enemy." He himself joined in the deception by asking a farmer questions about Staten Island and then—acting as if he had accidentally allowed information to pass—he said that his words should be treated with "the most profound Secrecy."

Washington knew that just the opposite would happen, because the farmer was a Tory who would quickly report the conversation to British officers.

Washington left a small force at his New Jersey headquarters and marched southward while still making moves that indicated he was planning to attack New York by taking Staten Island, then crossing into Manhattan. He had a great many boats rounded up so that British agents could see preparations for the invasion of Manhattan from Staten Island. In Chatham, New Jersey, he set up a big camp, complete with a bakery large enough to supply bread to an army. To Clinton, this was proof that Washington was establishing a base camp for his assault on New York.

Rochambeau's son, a colonel, broke security by telling his girlfriend that the American-French force was heading for Chesapeake Bay, where they would meet up with more French forces. The girlfriend was one of the best spies the British had, but fortunately for Washington, when her report reached Clinton, he did not believe it.

☼ ☼ ☼

Washington had another purpose for heading south. He was still determined to capture Benedict Arnold, whose Loyalists were on a rampage in Virginia, looting Richmond and raiding communities where Patriot supplies were stored. Washington sent American troops under the command of the Marquis de Lafayette to get Arnold.

The marquis was 19 when he left France and reported to General Washington in Philadelphia in 1777. Lafayette had reason to fight on America's side. When he was only two years old, his father had been killed in a battle against the British. Washington took an immediate liking to Lafayette, who looked upon Washington as the father he never knew.

Lafayette had been assigned a Virginia slave named James Armistead, whose master had given him permission to join the war. Armistead volunteered to spy on the British. He slipped through the British lines and found his way to Arnold's headquarters. Claiming to be an escaped slave, he said he would work as a servant or guide if the British would free him after they won the war. The British put him to work—as a spy.

A SLAVE BECOMES A SPY. James Armistead, spying for the Americans, convinces General Arnold that he will spy for the British.

Now a double agent, Armistead returned to Lafayette. On one mission, he carried back to the British a crumpled piece of paper that he said he had found. The false document indicated that American troops were on their way to Lafayette's camp. From New York to Virginia, American intelligence operatives like Armistead were bewildering the British. [1]

Lafayette failed to kidnap Arnold, who slipped

away and, in later raids in Connecticut, burned warehouses, ships, and much of New London. But Lafayette's maneuvers helped set up what would be the battle that ended the war.

✿ ✿ ✿

Clinton had ordered Cornwallis to establish a stronghold in Virginia. Cornwallis knew that he could only get supplies and reinforcements by sea because the Americans would block anything coming by land. So he set up his encampment at Yorktown at the tip of the York River peninsula on Chesapeake Bay. Lafayette, ordered to trap Cornwallis, sent Private Charles Morgan, playing the role of a deserter, into the British camp.

Morgan managed to talk directly to Cornwallis and to convince him that Lafayette had enough boats to cross the river in pursuit of the British. Mission completed, Morgan returned, in a Redcoat uniform, accompanied by six British soldiers—all true deserters, won over to the American army by Morgan. He also had in tow a Hessian prisoner.

Meanwhile, as Cornwallis had his men build defenses against an attack, he learned that 3,000

French troops had arrived to reinforce Lafayette's forces. Threatened on land, he still could take comfort from the fact that he could get aid from the sea. He knew that a British fleet under Admiral Thomas Graves was on its way to Yorktown from New York.

What Cornwallis did not know was that French ships under de Grasse now stood in the way. Graves's fleet could not reach Cornwallis without first breaking through the French fleet. On September 5, 1781, Admiral Graves's 19 warships reached the mouth of the Chesapeake. De Grasse's fleet of some two dozen ships sailed out of the bay to give battle. Fighting and maneuvering continued for days, with Admiral Graves giving orders by signal flags that sailors raised aloft on his flagship. Finally, Graves, realizing he could not win, gave the order to leave. His battered fleet limped back to New York.

Washington, Rochambeau, and Lafayette all met in Williamsburg on September 14. A few days later the main army, which had sailed down Chesapeake Bay, arrived. The combined force marched to Yorktown. Encircled by about 17,000 American and French soldiers, Cornwallis's 8,000 men were trapped. The siege lasted two weeks. On October 19 Cornwallis surrendered, ending the last major battle of the Revolutionary War. The surrender led to talks that ended the war in 1783.

✿ ✿ ✿

Back in the darkest of days in 1776, Washington had written, "There is one evil I dread, and that is, their spies." Out of that dread had come George Washington, spymaster. He built and ran an intelligence operation that helped him outwit his foe and win the war.

Even in that last battle, he had been well served by what he called the "honest, sensible and diligent men" of America's first intelligence service. Agents managed to intercept Cornwallis's encrypted reports to Clinton during the siege of Yorktown, and James Lovell cracked the code that Cornwallis used. These dispatches gave Washington valuable information about the ever-worsening condition of Cornwallis's army. In the battle between the British and French fleets in Chesapeake Bay, thanks to Washington's agents, the French may have been reading Admiral Graves's flag signals. Navies sent messages to each other by flags, which were visible for miles when hoisted high above the ships. The meaning of the flag signals—a certain flag or set of flags for commands such as "attack" or "hold your fire"—was a secret known only to those who had flag codebooks.

Remember James Rivington, the New York Tory who printed the pro-British *Gazette* and spied for Washington? Some historians believe that Rivington managed to get his hands on a copy of the flag signal codebook, which he passed to one of Washington's best operatives, the daring Allan McLane. Then, according to the handed-down story, McLane managed to somehow deliver the codebook to Admiral de Grasse, enabling him to foresee British maneuvers and win the sea battle. Details of Rivington's exploits, founded more on legend than on fact, remain mysterious. One theory makes him a British agent who decided to spy for the Americans after he saw that they would probably win the war.

When George Washington triumphantly entered New York City at the end of the war, he is said to have given Rivington a bag of gold—the typical payment to a hired spy, who works for gold, not out of

GEORGE WASHINGTON leads a victory parade in New York City. Later he will give a bag of gold to a valuable spy.

patriotism. Washington also stopped by the tailor shop of Hercules Mulligan and ordered a suit of civilian clothes. Mulligan thereafter called himself "Clothier to Genl. Washington," but the tailor did not advertise his other service to the general. And he did not take a bag of gold.

Other spies, including members of the Culper Ring, also kept their deeds secret, some for a lifetime, obeying the words of their spymaster: "There can be scarcely any need of recommending the greatest Caution and secrecy in a Business so critical and dangerous."

That caution and secrecy kept many spy stories from ever being made public. The names of many Patriots in the spy war will never be known. But it is no secret that they helped win the Revolutionary War. Nor is it a secret that George Washington was their superb spymaster. His skills were recognized by none other than Major George Beckwith, the head of British intelligence operations in America at the end of the war. Beckwith later noted: "Washington did not really outfight the British, he simply outspied us!"

BE IT REMEMBERED:

THAT on the 17th of October, 1781, Lieutenant-General Earl CORNWALLIS, with above Five thousand British Troops, surrendered themselves Prisoners of War to his Excellency Gen. GEORGE WASHINGTON, Commander in Chief of the allied Forces of France and America.

LAUS DEO:

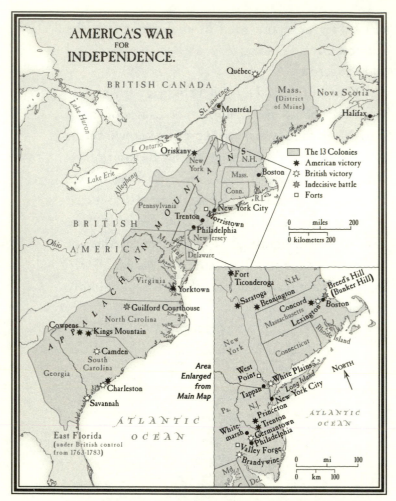

AMERICA'S WAR FOR INDEPENDENCE.

BRITISH CANADA

Québec

Mass. (District of Maine)

Nova Scotia

Halifax

Montréal

St. Lawrence

Lake Huron

L. Ontario

Oriskany

New York

N.H.

Mass.

Boston

Lake Erie

Alleghany

Conn.

R.I.

New York City

Pennsylvania

Trenton

Morristown

BRITISH

Ohio

AMERICAN

Philadelphia

New Jersey

Maryland

Delaware

Virginia

Yorktown

Guilford Courthouse

North Carolina

Cowpens

Kings Mountain

Camden

South Carolina

Georgia

Charleston

Savannah

East Florida
(under British control
from 1763-1783)

ATLANTIC OCEAN

| The 13 Colonies
✳ American victory
☆ British victory
✳ Indecisive battle
☐ Forts

0   miles   200

0   kilometers   200

Area Enlarged from Main Map

Fort Ticonderoga

N.H.

Breed's Hill (Bunker Hill)

Saratoga

Bennington

Concord

Boston

Lexington

Massachusetts

New York

Rhode Island

Connecticut

West Point

White Plains

NORTH

Tappan

Long Island

New York City

Pa.

N.J.

Princeton

ATLANTIC OCEAN

White-marsh

Trenton

Germantown

Philadelphia

Valley Forge

Brandywine

Md.

Del.

0   mi   100

0   km   100

MAJOR BATTLES OF THE REVOLUTION, with symbols indicating which were won by American or British forces and which resulted in outcomes that were not so clear, are shown on this map.

War
Time Line.

IN WHICH *the author*
lists some of the main events
pertaining to the Revolutionary War.

1763
- French and Indian War ends in victory for Britain.

1765
- Britain passes the Stamp Act.
- Sons of Liberty founded.

1768
- British troops land in Boston.

1770
- British troops and citizens clash in what Patriots call the Boston Massacre.

1773
- Sons of Liberty stage the Boston Tea Party to protest the Tea Act.

1774
- Quartering Act requires colonists to provide shelter for British troops.
- First Continental Congress assembles in Philadelphia.
- General Gage closes Massachusetts General Court.
- Massachusetts Provincial Congress recruits a 12,000-man militia and forms a Committee of Safety.

1775

- Patrick Henry delivers his "Give me liberty or give me death!" speech in Virginia's House of Burgesses.
- Paul Revere warns John Hancock and Samuel Adams to flee Lexington.
- Redcoats and Patriot militiamen clash at Lexington and Concord.
- Second Continental Congress meets in Philadelphia.
- Washington takes command of Continental Army; siege of Boston begins.
- British suffer heavy losses in Battle of Breed's (Bunker) Hill.
- Benedict Arnold and Ethan Allan take Fort Ticonderoga.

1776

- British evacuate Boston.
- Declaration of Independence is signed.
- British occupy the city of New York.
- Nathan Hale hanged by the British for spying.
- British defeat Benedict Arnold at Lake Champlain.
- British capture Fort Washington, in New York, and Fort Lee, in New Jersey.
- Washington crosses the Delaware River and captures Trenton, New Jersey.

1777

- Washington defeats British at Princeton, New Jersey.
- Fort Ticonderoga is retaken by the British.
- Congress flees Philadelphia; British occupy the city.
- British surrender at Saratoga, New York.
- Washington's army makes winter quarters at Valley Forge, Pennsylvania.

1778

- France decides to come to the aid of America.
- British leave Philadelphia, enter New York, and occupy it until the war ends.
- Washington sets up headquarters at White Plains, New York.

- British occupy Savannah, Georgia.
- French and American troops attack British forces in Newport, Rhode Island.

1779

- Off England, John Paul Jones wins a naval battle between his *Bon Homme Richard* and the Royal Navy's *Serapis*.
- British in Virginia capture and set fire to Portsmouth and Norfolk.
- Benedict Arnold becomes a spy for the British.
- British leave Rhode Island.

1780

- British capture Charleston, South Carolina.
- More French troops land in Newport, Rhode Island.
- John André is hanged as a British spy.
- Benedict Arnold becomes a British general.

1781

- Articles of Confederation are adopted.

- French troops leave Rhode Island and join Washington's army in New York.
- British fleet is driven off by French warships in Chesapeake Bay.
- American-French force under Washington and Rochambeau besieges the army of British General Charles Cornwallis at Yorktown, Virginia.
- Cornwallis surrenders; British government realizes that this means the end of the war.

1782

- British government begins peace talks.
- Americans and British agree on a peace treaty.

1783

- Great Britain and the United States sign the peace treaty in Paris.
- Tens of thousands of Loyalists leave the United States; most of them move to Canada and England.

Spy Talk.

IN WHICH *the author
defines spy terms
used in his book.*

AGENT — a spy under the control of an *intelligence officer.*

CIPHER — a way to make a message secret by changing one letter for another.

CODE — a way to make a message secret by replacing words or phrases with other words or numbers.

COMMITTEE FOR SECRET CORRESPONDENCE — the first American spy organization. Ben Franklin used it to run *covert operations* in France.

COUNTERSPY — an agent whose job is to find out about spying being done by the enemy and figure out ways to stop it.

COVER — a fake identity used by an *agent.*

COVERT OPERATION — a secret activity carried out in a way that cannot be traced back to the people really running it.

CUT-OUT — a third person used to conceal the contact between two other people—usually an agent and the intelligence officer handling the agent.

DEAD DROP — a place where the *agent* and his *intelligence officer* can leave and pick up messages or packages without making personal contact with each other.

DISINFORMATION — false information created by one side to fool the other. It is deliberately passed to the enemy.

DOUBLE AGENT — an *agent* who works for one side while at the same time secretly working for the other side.

INTELLIGENCE OFFICER — a person who supervises, or "runs," agents.

MOLE — an *agent* who operates inside the enemy's government, military organization, or intelligence service. Usually, a mole holds an important post.

SAFE HOUSE — a place where an *intelligence officer* and *agent* can secretly meet without fear of being seen by the other side. The safe house usually is owned, leased, or occupied by a trusted helper of the intelligence officer.

STAY-BEHIND AGENT — an *agent* who remains in an area that has passed into the control of the other side. Usually, the stay-behind agent has a *cover*, such as being a grocer. Communications with an intelligence officer is risky and difficult, but the stay-behind agent provides valuable information that can only come from someone on the scene.

Appendix III.

The Code.*

IN WHICH *the reader learns
how to decipher the numbers
in Tallmadge's code.*

*To find this code online, key in "George Washington Papers at Library of Congress,"
search "codes," and select "Talmadge, 1783, codes." (Note the alternate spelling of
"Tallmadge.") The use of a "?" in the code printed here indicates where Tallmadge's
handwriting was not readable. Spellings and abbreviations are as they appear in the code.

✿ ✿ ✿

✿ ✿ ✿

161

164

s . . . . u	z . . . . t	5 . . . . k
t v		6 . . . . m
u . . . . w	*Numbers*	7 . . . . n
v x	1 . . . . e	8 . . . . o
w . . . . y	2 . . . . f	9 . . . . q
x . . . . z	3 . . . . g	0 . . . . u
y . . . . s	4 i	

TALLMADGE'S DIRECTIONS FOR THE ALPHABET

N.B. the use of this alphabet is when you wish to express some words not
mentioned in the numerical Dictionary. For instance the word heart. would
be expressed thus biely. look [at] the letters of the real word in the first
column of the alphabet and then opposite to them, let those letters in the
second column represent them; in this case always observe to draw a line
under the word, as fwv. stands for but

Numbers are represented by their opposite letters which must have a double line under them as fikm is 2456. & nqu is 790 . . .

TALLMADGE'S DIRECTIONS FOR THE NUMERICAL DICTIONARY.

In the numerical Dictionary it is sufficient to express a part of a sentence
only in figures, to make the rest perfectly unintelligible, as all words cannot be mentioned ? & synonimous meaning must be sought for & if not to
be found, & the word not proper to be wrote, then the alphabet must be
used—when numbers are used always observe to put a period after the number thus 284. stands for it and 295. inforce.

It will often happen that the same word may need to be changed thro the
different moods, tenses, ? thus if you would express the word Introduce
the number would be 328. if you would express the word introduced make
a small flourish over the same 328—Horse is repres. by 255. Horses by 255.
kill by 344. killed by 344. impress by 290. impressed by 290. in such cases
the foregoing & subsequent parts must determine the word.

GEORGE WASHINGTON'S DESK at Mount Vernon awaited him at war's end. During the war he wrote many documents, including secret orders to spies.

Text Notes.

IN WHICH *the author*
provides additional information
about people and events in his book.

CHAPTER 1: BIRTH OF A SPYMASTER.

[1] Christopher Gist explored the Ohio River from its source near Shannopin's Town, Pennsylvania (today's Pittsburgh), to the stretch of land that became Louisville, Kentucky. He opened Kentucky to settlement by colonists, although credit for this is usually given to his neighbor, Daniel Boone, who reached Kentucky in 1767. One of Gist's sons married a sister of a Cherokee chief. They became the parents of Sequoyah, who created the Cherokee alphabet.

[2] George Washington's journal was published in *The Maryland Gazette* in March 1754. You can read it at http://earlyamerica.com/earlyamerica/milestones/journal or in his handwriting online at The George Washington Papers at the Library of Congress.

CHAPTER 2: SPY AGAINST SPY.

[1] The French and Indian War was part of a worldwide conflict known as the Seven Years War (1756–1763), which was fought not only in North America but also in Europe and India. The two major foes were France

and Great Britain, which at the time included England, Scotland, and Wales. (In this book we have used "England" because most British forces in America were from England.) By 1763, the nations were tired of war and, under a peace agreement, France gave up all of its claims on the mainland of North America. Great Britain's holdings became so widespread that it was said the sun never set on the British Empire.

[2] The identity of the waitress is not known. We do know about the spies' mission because, after the British evacuated Boston in March 1776, some Patriots found a copy of the mission report and had it "printed for the information and amusement of the curious."

[3] When the British marched to Concord, frightened women and children fled to the home of the Reverend William Emerson. His grandson, Ralph Waldo Emerson, would write a famous poem telling how "embattled farmers stood, / And fired the shot heard round the world."

CHAPTER 3: A SPY MUST DIE.

[1] George Hewes, who lived to be almost 100, was one of the last survivors of the Boston Massacre. A Boston shoemaker, he became a Patriot after seeing his shop "pulled down and burned by British troops." Historians still do not know what intelligence he gave to Washington.

[2] We have more evidence of Church's spying than Washington did. Letters now in the William L. Clements Libary at the University of Michigan show that he had passed information to General Gage six weeks before the battle of Lexington. (Visit the collection online: http://www.si.umich.edu/spies/)

[3] Since Congress had not passed any laws about the penalty for spying, George Washington used military tribunals (court martials) rather than civilian courts to try accused spies. As commander-in-chief, he could determine their punishment.

[4] Today's Army Rangers, Special Forces, and Delta Force trace their origins to Knowlton's Rangers. This unit was the first American military intelligence organization.

[5] A Connecticut Tory, Consider Tiffany, wrote a history of the Revolution. His family kept the manuscript until 2000, when G. Bradford

Tiffany donated it to the Library of Congress. The account "fits the facts as we know them" and "one is tempted to accept it as being substantially true," says James H. Hutson of the Library of Congress. "Tiffany's story reflects badly on Nathan Hale's judgment, but...does not diminish his patriotism."

CHAPTER 4: GEORGE WASHINGTON, AGENT 711.

[1] During the war, Honeyman lived a protected life, helped in secret ways. In 1777 he was arrested and charged with treason by officials of the Patriot government of New Jersey. He was not convicted; nor did anything come of a similar charge in 1778. And when New Jersey officials were selling off the property of Tories, the scheduled sale of Honeyman's possessions never happened. When the war ended, Washington publicly revealed Honeyman's patriotic work and personally thanked him.

[2] Long after the war, Tallmadge wrote a recollection of his military service, but all he says about what he did for Washington is "I kept one or more boats continually employed in crossing the [Long Island] Sound on this business." What we know comes from other sources, including documents written by George Washington.

[3] No one knew Townsend's real name until 1930, when historian Morton Pennypacker asked a handwriting expert to match the handwriting of "Culper Jr." with handwriting known to be Townsend's. Rivington, hated as a Tory after the war, lost his business and died in poverty. In 1959, another historian, Catherine Snell Crary of Finch College, proved that Rivington actually spied for Washington. He may have kept his secret after the war to protect his two sons serving in the British Army.

[4] One of the committee's counterspies was Enoch Crosby, who is believed to be the model for "Harvey Birch" in James Fenimore Cooper's novel *The Spy*. John Jay told Cooper about Crosby's exploits as a fake Tory.

[5] John Jay worked closely with Washington on intelligence and counterintelligence operations. But they disagreed on the question of how secret those operations should be. Washington thought that army and civilian morale would be raised if some intelligence victories were revealed. But Jay held firm that intelligence "is unfortunately of such

a Nature . . . as to render Secrecy necessary." Jay won the argument.

CHAPTER 5: TOOLS OF THE SPYMASTER.

[1] In the visible letter Benjamin Thompson gives information he says he received from a "Field officer in the Rebel Army (if that mass of confusion may be called an Army)." The invisible letter instructs the courier to deliver the letter and "the Papers which I left in your care, and take his Receipt for the same." We don't know who the papers were delivered to, since Thompson did not write a name anywhere on the letter. He just told the letter courier where to take it. The "Papers" may have been documents he took from the desk of Dr. Benjamin Church, the mole in the Sons of Liberty. For the full text of the visible and invisible letters, see http://www.si.umich.edu/spies/letter-1775may6-1.html.

[2] Clinton's letter with mask in place looked like this:

"You will have heard, Dr **Sir** I doubt not long before this can have reached you that Sir **W. Howe** is gone from hence. The Rebels imagine that he **is gone to the** Eastward. By this time however he has filled **Chesapeak bay with** surprize and terror. Washington marched **the greater part of the** Rebels to Philadelphia in order to oppose Sir Wm's. **army. I hear he is** now returned upon finding none of our troops **landed but am not** sure of this, great part of his troops are returned for **certain. I am** sure this countermarching must be ruin to them. I am **left to command** here, half of my force may I am sure defend everything **here with** much safety. I shall therefore send Sir W. 4 or 5 Bat [talio] ns. I have **too small a force** to invade the New England provinces; they are too weak **to make any effectual** efforts against me and you do not want any **diversion in your favour.** I can, therefore very well spare him 1500 men. **I shall try some thing** certainly towards the close of the year, not till then **at any rate.** It may be of use to inform you that report says all yields **to you.** I own to you that **I think** the business will quickly be over now. **Sr. W's move just at this time** has been capital. Washingtons have been **the worst he could take** in every respect. sincerely give you **much joy on your success** and am with great Sincerity your [ ] / HC

170

[3] Howe in his message sent in a quill pen says he is going to invade "Pensilvania" and will not be moving up the Hudson to join Burgoyne.

[4] A strange monument marks Arnold as a hero, not a traitor. The monument, to his leg, stands at Saratoga National Historic Park.

[5] Committees of Safety, an idea imported from England, were set up by Colonies (and sometimes by communities) to take charge of the militia and its supplies. As the Revolution neared, many Committees of Safety took on intelligence-gathering missions.

[6] The story of Alexander Bryan's mission was revealed by his son, Daniel, in 1852. Daniel said his father told him that General Gates had promised to send a doctor to care for his wife and son. But Gates broke his promise. The son died. Neighbors failed to help Mrs. Bryan because they believed that Bryan had fled to the British side.

CHAPTER 6: FRANKLIN'S FRENCH FRIENDS.

[1] In 1777, the Committee of Secret Correspondence was renamed the Committee of Foreign Affairs, but it kept its intelligence role.

[2] Two members of the Lee family signed the Declaration of Independence—Richard Henry Lee and Francis Lightfoot Lee; "Light Horse Harry" Lee, a hero of the Revolutionary War, was the father of Robert E. Lee, who would command the Confederate Army in the Civil War.

[3] Bancroft's spying finally became known in 1889, when documents of the British Secret Service were published in America.

CHAPTER 7: SPYMASTER AT WORK.

[1] The "flat-bottomed boats" that Sackett's spy saw were also known as "Durham boats," after Robert Durham, a Pennsylvania engineer. Typically, each was about 35 feet long and could carry up to 1,500 pounds of cargo. They could be propelled by long oars, by sails, or by poling.

[2] According to John Bakeless in *Turncoats, Traitors and Heroes,* "Old Mom" Rinker "was often suspected of doing exactly what she was doing, but she acted her role so well, suspicion did no harm."

[3] The Philadelphia Quakers later asked Charles Darragh to leave the Friends Meeting because he had fought in the war. Some sources say

that Lydia Darragh was expelled for her activities. The story of the spying, told by Lydia's daughter, Ann, was published in 1827.

[4] Washington reported spending $6,170 for spying in Philadelphia. (That would be worth about $140,000 today.) There is no indication that Lydia Darragh got any money for her work.

CHAPTER 8: THE GENERAL IS A SPY.

[1] Benedict Arnold gave himself the code name "Monk," after George Monk, a 17th-century British general who helped to overthrow Parliament and put Charles II on the throne.

[2] To read the decoded version of the letter Arnold wrote to André on July 15, 1780, go online to the Gallery of Letters in the Clements Library at http://www.si.umich.edu/spies/index-gallery.html.

[3] André was buried in a grave in Tappan. In 1821 gravediggers unearthed his remains (killing a peach tree because its roots had become wrapped around his skull). The remains were shipped to London and placed before a large memorial to him in Westminster Abbey.

[4] The name of the second man is not known. Champe had to have him to carry out the plan. "Champe and his friend," according to Lee's account, "intended to have placed themselves each under Arnold's shoulder, and to have thus borne him through the most unfrequented alleys and streets to the boat; representing Arnold, in case of being questioned, as a drunken soldier whom they were conveying to the guard-house."

[5] Arnold learned in England that no one trusts a traitor. When he left the British Army he could not find a job. He moved his family to Canada and started a shipping business. Even among the Tories of Canada he could not find friends or trust. He took his family back to London, where he unsuccessfully tried to get a commission again in the British Army. In 1801, he died, bitter and still distrusted.

CHAPTER 9: VICTORY IN THE SPY WAR.

[1] Armistead was granted his freedom by the Virginia legislature as a reward for his work as an American spy.

Quote Sources.

IN WHICH *quotes are listed*
by chapter and page number
and their sources are revealed. *

CHAPTER 1: BIRTH OF A SPYMASTER.

pp. 5–13 all quotes from "A Journal of my Journey over the Mountains..."
online in The George Washington Papers, Library of Congress.

CHAPTER 2: SPY AGAINST SPY.

p. 16 "I escaped...me." from Washington's letter, Smithsonian Web site:
http://www.georgewashington.si.edu/life/chrono_military.html; p. 17
"There is...obtain." from Washington's letter to Robert Morris January 1, 1756,
The George Washington Papers, Library of Congress; and "such an ...Com-
panion" at http://www.georgewashington.si.edu/life/chrono_mili-
tary.html; pp. 18–19 "defense of...birthright" from Thomas Jefferson's paper,
"Declaration of Causes of Taking Up Arms;" p. 25 "the doors...secret"

---

*Full bibliographic information is listed only after the first reference or for sources
not listed in Further Reading on pages 178–79. Many of George Washington's
quotes can be viewed online in his handwriting in The George Washington Papers at
the Library of Congress by searching phrases from the quote.

from Carl G. Karsch, "The First Continental Congress: A Dangerous Journey Begins" on http://www.ushistory.org/carpentershall/history/congress.htm; p. 26 "powder and cartridges" and "sudden blow" in the "Notes of Royal Commission on Losses and Services of American Loyalists," edited by H. E. Egerton; p. 29 "heavy fire...Barns, etc." in *A New Age Now Begins*, by Page Smith, published by McGraw-Hill, 1976, Vol. 1, p. 485.

CHAPTER 3: A SPY MUST DIE.
p. 31 "to go...designs" from The George Washington Papers, Library of Congress; p. 32 "No danger...South Carolina" in the Gage Papers, Clements Library, University of Michigan http://www.si.umich.edu; pp. 33–34 "immediate...war" from the original letters published in *Memoirs of the American Revolution*, by John Drayton, published by Ayer Co., 1969; p. 35 "I immediately...author" in *Secret History of the American Revolution*, by Carl Van Doren, published by Viking Press, 1978, p. 20; p. 37 "holding...enemy" *Honorable Treachery*, p. 15 ; p. 40 "mutiny,...Army" in *American Archives*, Peter Force, ed., 4th series, 6:1146; and "by water... day" from *Honorable Treachery*, p. 21; p. 41 "I am...undertake it" in *Captain Nathan Hale and Major John Palsgrave Wyllys*, by George Dudley Seymour, published by Tuttle, Morehouse & Taylor, 1933, p. 25; p. 43 "I only...country" from *Spy Book: The Encyclopedia of Espionage*, "Nathan Hale."

CHAPTER 4: GEORGE WASHINGTON, AGENT 711.
p. 45 "I think...up" quoted in "A Spy for Washington," by Leonard Falkner, in *American Heritage*, August, 1957, p. 59; p. 47 "an army of farmers," Ibid., p. 61; p. 49 "protected...a spy" Ibid.,p. 62; pp. 50–51 "was a large,...purpose" a quote from William Patchin in "Leading the Charge" by George De Wan on http://www.newsday.com/extras/lihistory; p. 51 "the health...opinion" *Turncoats, Traitors, and Heroes*, p. 218; p. 52 "I opened a...New York" *Memoir of Colonel Benjamin Tallmadge*, prepared by Benjamin Tallmadge, 1858, reissued by Arno Press, 1968, p. 29; p. 52 "mix...observations" in *Spy Book: The Encyclopedia of Espionage*, p. 151; p. 54 "for your ...business" from a letter on the Spy Museum Web site www.spymuseum.org; p. 56 "surreptitious...enemy" "Washington's Eyes and Ears" by George De Wan,

http://www.newsday.com/extras/lihistory; pp. 56–57 "There is one...Intelligence" Marks' reports in Clinton Papers, Clements Library, University of Michigan. The British agent is quoted in *Magazine of American History,* Vol. 10, p. 413; p. 57 "Private dispatches...certain woman's" Ibid., Vol. 10, p. 413; p. 58 "Gow & lie...mails" *Spying for America,* pp. 23–24; p. 59 "the fashionable clothier" from Biography of Hercules Mulligan in "Notable Irish-Americans" http://www.irishisle.com; p. 60 "a sensible...double spies" in The George Washington Papers, Library of Congress; p. 61 "intended to fall...Hands" Ibid.; and "are very...regiments" Ibid.; and "wilderness...merge" *Spy Book: The Encyclopedia of Espionage,* p. 595.

CHAPTER 5: TOOLS OF THE SPYMASTER.

pp. 64–65 letters are in George De Wan's "Crafty Codes of American Spies" http://www.lihistory.com; pp. 65–66 "communications...fears" in "Intelligence in the War of Independence: Secret Writing" http://www.opsec.org/opsnews/Sept99/opssecretsept99.htm; p. 66 "convey...me" quoted in "Document J" on http://www.bhsonline.org/library/Teachers/kelleher/DBQMilitary Intelligence; p. 67 "one of your...cleaning" letter shown on http:// www.si.umich.edu/spies/letter; p. 69 "would elude...counterpart" *U.S. Revolutionary Period Cryptography,* Signal Security Agency, Aegean Park Press, 1999, pp. 11–12; pp. 69–70 "[H]e should...small value" *General Washington's Spies on Long Island and in New York,* by Morton Pennypacker, published by the Long Island Historical Society, N.Y., 1939, pp. 58–59; p. 70 "much better...sheet" from Washington's letter to Tallmadge Februrary 5, 1780, The George Washington Papers, Library of Congress; p. 71 "friends of...Government" from General Howe's letter to Sir Guy Carleton, in *A New Age Now Begins,* Vol. 2, p. 892; p. 73 "I am lost...Gates" from "Daniel Taylor, the Spy," by John M. Eager, *History Magazine,* Vol. 8, pp. 149–150; p. 75 "the best ...enterprise" in "Reminiscences of Saratoga and Ballston," by William L. Stone on http://www.rootsweb.com/~nysarato/stone/chap07.html.

CHAPTER 6: FRANKLIN'S FRENCH FRIENDS.

p. 77 "for the sole...the world" from *Encyclopedia of the American Revo-*

lution, by Mark M. Boatner, published by D. McKay Co., 1975; p. 79 "and other foreigners" from *Intelligence in the War of Independence,* p. 23; p. 80 "hard money" and "to pay...half crown" letter from Washington to Robert Morris in The George Washington Papers, Library of Congress; pp. 81–82 "We haves...no blankets" from http://www. american revolution. org/fr7.html; p. 85 "strutted...plaything" from *Spying for America,* p. 38; p. 86 "was erected...next" author interview with curator for the Portsmouth Historic Dockyard; p. 88 "the independency...power" Bancroft's letter http://www.fas.org.ciReader; p. 89 "the progress...materials" Ibid; p. 91 "jealous,...quarrelsome" from a Franklin letter in *A New Age Now Begins,* Vol. 2, p. 1139; p. 92 "as if...enemies" from *Spying for America,* p. 48.

CHAPTER 7: SPYMASTER AT WORK.

p. 95 "the wife...enemy" from Sackett's letter to Washington, April 7, 1777, International Spy Museum, Washington, D.C.; p. 96 "subdue that city" from Sackett's letter to Washington, April 7, 1777; p. 97 "on spy service" from Clark's report to Washington, The George Washington Papers, Library of Congress; p. 99 "persons...divulge" in the George Washington Papers, Library of Congress; p. 100 "risque my all...intelligence" in *Writings of George Washington,* edited by J.C. Fitzpatrick, published by the USGPO, 1933–44; p. 101 "proper persons" Ibid., Vol. 7, p. 462; p. 102 "might prove...our cause" Washington to Nathanael Greene, quoted in *A New Age Now Begins,* Vol. 2, p. 990; pp. 105–06 "This morning...move" from Clark's report in *The Historical Society of Pennsylvania Bulletin,* Vol. 1, p. 22; p. 106 "better...designs" quoted in *Intelligence in the War of Independence,* "Washington's Intelligence Officers" at http://www.cia.gov/cia/ publications/ warindep/pers.shtm#wash; pp. 107–08 "little poor-looking...headquarters" Boudinot's memoir at http://www.ushistory. org/march/bio/lydia.htm; pp. 108–09 "a country girl...fear" in *Memoir of Colonel Benjamin Tallmadge,* pp. 26–27; p. 110 "One thing...ears" Boudinot's memoir on http://www.ushistory.org/march/bio/lydia.htm; p. 111 "finished or unfinished" from *Washington, the Indispensable Man,* by James Thomas Flexner, published by Little, Brown, 1974, p. 119.

✿ ✿ ✿

CHAPTER 8: THE GENERAL IS A SPY.

p. 114 "communicated...British forces" *A New Age Now Begins*, Smith, Vol. 2, p. 1560; p. 115 "I went...New York" Ibid., Vol. 2, p. 1560; p. 116 "Three ...Word" from Andre's May 10, 1779, letter to Stansbury at http://www.si.umich.edu/spies/index-gallery.html; pp.116–17 Ibid., July 12, 1780, letter; p. 120 "some secret...kept a secret" from *Turncoats, Traitors, and Heroes*, p. 289; p. 121 "a person...New York" from *General Washington's Spies on Long Island and in New York*, p. 117; p. 124 "I searched...paper" from *History Magazine*, Vol. 1, Nov. 1857, pp. 331–336; p. 126 "particular...Washington" *A New Age Now Begins*, Vol. 2, p. 1584; p. 127 "Great Arnold...feeling" traditional accounts of Washington's reaction; and "retaliate ...my Power" in *The Secret History of the American Revolution*, by Carl Van Doren, pp. 490–491; p. 128 "I pray...man" *A New Age Now Begins*, Vol. 2, p. 1593; and "full of bone...plan" in *Memoirs of the War in the Southern Department of the United States*, by Henry Lee, with new introduction by Charles Royster, published by Da Capo Press, 1998; p. 129 "put spur...escaped" Ibid.; p. 130 "one for...approached" Ibid.; p. 131 "this...traitors" quoted in *Intelligence in the War for Independence*, p. 18.

CHAPTER 9: VICTORY IN THE SPY WAR.

p. 134 "an attack...whole" in *Turncoats, Traitors, and Heroes*, p. 330; p. 135 "As we may...importance" in *General Washington's Spies on Long Island and in New York*, p. 78; p. 136 "news...consequence" quoted in "A ruse Saves the French Fleet," by George De Wan, http://www.newsday.com/extras/lihistory/4/hs414a.htm; pp. 136–37 "Sir....country" Ibid.; p. 140 "If we...Secrecy" in *Recollections and Private Memoirs of Washington*, published by J. W. Bradley, 1861, pp. 230 ff.; p. 146 "There is one...spies" quoted at http://www.cia.gov/cia/publications/warind/frames; p. 146 "honest...men" Ibid.; p. 148 "Clothier to Genl. Washington" in *Hercules Mulligan: Confidential Correspondent of George Washington*, by Michael J. O'Brien, published by P.J. Kennedy, 1937, pp. 49, 85; pp. 148–49 "There can...dangerous" in *General Washington's Spies on Long Island and in New York*, p. 49; p. 149 "Washington...outspied us!" quoted by Delia M. Rios on http://www.newhousenews.com/archive/story/a041702.

Appendix VI.

Further Reading.

IN WHICH *the author*
suggests sources for learning
more about espionage
in the American Revolution.*

Turncoats, Traitors, and Heroes: Espionage in the American Revolution,
by John Edwin Bakeless, published by Da Capo Press, 1998.
Bakeless, who once served in U.S. Army intelligence, spent nearly 20
years gathering information for the book, which was first published in
1959. The book is a book of discovery—for him and for the reader.

Honorable Treachery: A History of U.S. Intelligence, Espionage, and
Covert Action from the American Revolution to the CIA, by
George J. A. O'Toole, published by Atlantic Monthly Press, 1991.
O'Toole was a CIA intelligence officer. In his chapters on the Revolutionary War, he showed that George Washington "recruited spies,
instructed them in their treacherous craft, sent them out, welcomed
them back, and paid them off."

---

*The books listed here were written for adults but are worth a look. Children's books
are listed on the CIA's Homepage for Kids *(see page 179)*.

Spying for America: The Hidden History of U.S. Intelligence, by
    Nathan Miller, published by Marlowe & Company, 1989.
    Miller writes about spying from the Revolutionary War to the Cold
    War. Although he does not have a connection with the CIA, as O'Toole
    had, he does give an interesting history of American intelligence.

Spy Book: The Encyclopedia of Espionage, by Norman Polmar and
    Thomas B. Allen, published by Random House, 1997.
    Included in the more than 2,000 entries in this book are essays on Amer-
    ican espionage and spy biographies of George Washington, Ben Franklin,
    and other people you met in this book.

Intelligence in the War of Independence
    This is not a book you can find in a bookstore or in the typical library.
    It was published by the Central Intelligence Agency (CIA) and can be
    found on the Internet at
    http://www.cia.gov/cia/publications/warindep/intro.shtml

Central Intelligence Agency Homepage for Kids
    Go to http://www.cia.gov/cia/ciakids/ to see what the CIA has to
    offer about espionage and its history. To learn about the CIA's view of
    George Washington, spymaster, go to
    http://www.cia.gov/cia/publications/warindep/pers.html

To see more spy letters of the Revolutionary War, go to
http://www.si.umich.edu/spies/

For a list of secrecy-related Web sites, check out the Federation of American Scientists online at:
http://www.fas.org/sgp/index.html

The National Security Agency's National Cryptologic Museum has inter-
esting information about codes and ciphers. Visit the Web site at:
http://www.NSA.gov/museum/index.html.

The Index.

IN WHICH *subjects*
are listed by page number, and
illustrations are indicated by italic type.

SECRETS CODES THROUGHOUT THIS BOOK.

Wondering why this page is numbered 721? Decipher the code below using the Culper code on pages 157–165 to find out.

23. fipdencp vemmnehaiu gqhi 411. 681. nfe

Use the "book code" described on pages 115–116 to solve the spy puzzle below.

125.4.6. 4.20.4. 143.1.4. 95.5.1. have 146.16.2. the 115.20.9. 54.21.8. 121.8.3. be a 142.23.5. 122.16.5. 128.22.3. can 34.9.7. 5.2.9. 116.2.6. 35.14.11. to 65.19.4. and 127.20.1. 70.10.1. 91.20.5. 67.6.11. 51.18.2. 56.22.2. 66.1.4. 19.15.6. this 108.3.6. 141.1.4. as 13.23.8. 23.20.4. 8.18.6. 93.10.3. 69.19.3. 120.16.2.

NOTE: To decipher the other codes hidden throughout the book, use the Culper code. To check your answers, visit the author's Web site: www.tballen.com.

ABOUT THE DESIGN OF THIS BOOK.

The design of this book is meant to take you back to the days when George Washington, Benjamin Franklin, and other Founding Fathers were using printed leaflets to spread the word about the revolution they were leading against England. This book is set in a type-

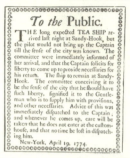

To the Public.

THE long expected TEA SHIP arrived last night at Sandy-Hook, but the pilot would not bring up the Captain till the sense of the city was known. The committee were immediately informed of her arrival, and that the Captain solicits for liberty to come up to provide necessaries for his return. The ship to remain at Sandy-Hook. The committee conceiving it to be the sense of the city that he should have such liberty, signified it to the Gentleman who is to supply him with provisions, and other necessaries. Advice of this was immediately dispatched to the Captain; and whenever he comes up, care will be taken that he does not enter at the custom-house, and that no time be lost in dispatching him.

New-York, April 19. 1774.

face called Caslon Antique. It is a digital version of the Caslon type-face used in the public notice (circa. 1774) shown here. The original typeface was designed in the early 1720s by an Englishman named William Caslon, a gunsmith turned type designer. It soon became the rage throughout Europe and the American Colonies. Used for early printings of The Declaration of Independence and later for The Constitution, it is sometimes referred to as the Freedom Font. The designer of the modern version used in this book is a mystery.

One of the most noticable differences in style between the old and the new Caslon is the treatment of the letter s. Note that it is sometimes elongated in the public notice. For the ease of the modern reader, we did not use the elongated s in this book, but we did incorporate other antique typesetting styles, such as the use of periods at the end of titles. You might be surprised to know that the old, broken looking type has the same distressed look as the type George Washington would have read. In Washington's time each letter was "punched" out of a piece of metal rather than being typeset on a computer as this book was. Back then, each letter was handmade into a lead mold that was placed in a tray with other letters and spaces on the printing press. Ink was rolled onto the letters, then paper was pressed onto the inked letters so that each left a slight depression in the paper. The imperfections of making tiny letters by hand out of metal and stamping them onto very textured paper is what created the "distressed" look. We simulated the depression the lead type made in the paper on this book's dust jacket. If you run your finger over the type, you'll discover that the letters sink slightly into the paper.

✿ ✿ ✿

ABOUT THE NATIONAL GEOGRAPHIC SOCIETY.

One of the world's largest nonprofit scientific and educational organizations, the National Geographic Society was founded in 1888 "for the increase and diffusion of geographic knowledge." Fulfilling this mission, the Society educates and inspires millions every day through its magazines, books, television programs, videos, maps and atlases, research grants, the National Geographic Bee, teacher workshops, and innovative classroom materials. The Society is supported through membership dues, charitable gifts, and income from the sale of its educational products. This support is vital to National Geographic's mission to increase global understanding and promote conservation of our planet through exploration, research, and education.

For more information, please call 1-800-NGS LINE (647-5463) or write to the following address:

NATIONAL GEOGRAPHIC SOCIETY
1145 17th Street N.W.
Washington, D.C. 20036-4688 U.S.A.
Visit the Society's Web site at www.nationalgeographic.com.